Guest-Edited by
TERRI PETERS

DESIGN
FOR HEALTH

Sustainable Approaches to Therapeutic Architecture

Profile
No 246

ARCHITECTURAL DESIGN
March/April 2017

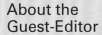
ISSN 0003-8504
ISBN 978-1119-162131

Sean Ahlquist, Costanza Colombi, Leah Ketcheson, Oliver Popadich and Disha Sharmin, Sensory Playscape - textile hybrid structure, Southern Illinois University, Carbondale, Illinois, 2016

Montgomery Sisam Architects with Farrow Partnership Architects, St John's Rehab, Sunnybrook Health Sciences, Toronto, 2010

Editorial Offices
John Wiley & Sons
9600 Garsington Road
Oxford
OX4 2DQ

T +44 (0)1865 776868

Consultant Editor
Helen Castle

Managing Editor
Caroline Ellerby
Caroline Ellerby Publishing

Freelance Contributing Editor
Abigail Grater

Publisher
Paul Sayer

Art Direction + Design
CHK Design:
Christian Küsters
Christos Kontogeorgos

Production Editor
Elizabeth Gongde

Prepress
Artmedia, London

Printed in Italy by Printer
Trento Srl

ⅅ ARCHITECTURAL DESIGN

March/April
2017

Profile No.
246

Front cover and inside
front cover: CF Møller,
Hospice Djursland,
Rønde, Denmark 2011.
© CF Møller/Adam Mørk

02/2017

Journal Customer Services
For ordering information,
claims and any enquiry
concerning your journal
subscription please go to
www.wileycustomerhelp
.com/ask or contact your
nearest office.

Americas
E: cs-journals@wiley.com
T: +1 781 388 8598 or
+1 800 835 6770 (toll free
in the USA & Canada)

**Europe, Middle East
and Africa**
E: cs-journals@wiley.com
T: +44 (0)1865 778315

Asia Pacific
E: cs-journals@wiley.com
T: +65 6511 8000

Japan (for Japanese-
speaking support)
E: cs-japan@wiley.com
T: +65 6511 8010 or 005 316
50 480 (toll-free)

Visit our Online Customer
Help available in 7 languages
at www.wileycustomerhelp
.com/ask

Print ISSN: 0003-8504
Online ISSN: 1554-2769

Prices are for six issues
and include postage and
handling charges. Individual-
rate subscriptions must be
paid by personal cheque or
credit card. Individual-rate
subscriptions may not be
resold or used as library
copies.

All prices are subject to
change without notice.

Identification Statement
Periodicals Postage paid
at Rahway, NJ 07065.
Air freight and mailing in
the USA by Mercury Media
Processing, 1850 Elizabeth
Avenue, Suite C, Rahway,
NJ 07065, USA.

USA Postmaster
Please send address changes
to *Architectural Design*,
John Wiley & Sons Inc.,
c/o The Sheridan Press,
PO Box 465, Hanover,
PA 17331, USA

Rights and Permissions
Requests to the Publisher
should be addressed to:
Permissions Department
John Wiley & Sons Ltd
The Atrium
Southern Gate
Chichester
West Sussex PO19 8SQ
UK

F: +44 (0)1243 770 620
E: Permissions@wiley.com

Subscribe to ⅅ
ⅅ is published bimonthly
and is available to purchase
on both a subscription basis
and as individual volumes
at the following prices.

Prices
Individual copies:
£24.99 / US$39.95
Individual issues on
ⅅ App for iPad:
£9.99 / US$13.99
Mailing fees for print
may apply

Annual Subscription Rates
Student: £84 / US$129
print only
Personal: £128 / US$201
print and iPad access
Institutional: £275 / US$516
print or online
Institutional: £330 / US$620
combined print and online
6-issue subscription on
ⅅ App for iPad: £44.99 /
US$64.99

Terri Peters is an architect, writer and researcher whose interdisciplinary work maps new trajectories of ecological design through contemporary practice, academic research and pop culture. She is an expert in sustainable architecture and her research focuses on the architectural and social implications of sustainable buildings, with a focus on qualitative parameters and wellbeing. She has a global perspective, having lived and worked in Vancouver, Tokyo, Paris, Copenhagen and London, which was her adopted home for eight years. After 12 years abroad she is currently back in her native Canada, as a post-doctoral researcher at the University of Toronto investigating the intersections of environmental design and wellbeing.

Her practice of architecture involves critical investigation and reflection from multiple angles. She has degrees in architectural history and environmental design, a professional degree in architecture, and a postgraduate diploma in professional practice. She has published more than 200 articles for specialist architecture and design magazines, and is a registered architect in the UK. She guest-edited the △ *Experimental Green Strategies: Redefining Ecological Design Research* (November/December 2011) issue, which defined and examined an emerging trend in contemporary architectural practice relating to the formation of sustainable design research groups. These groups mark a shift in how environmental design is approached in practice, and how ecological research is coming to be valued within the profession.

From 2009 to 2015 she was a PhD Fellow at Aarhus School of Architecture in Denmark, researching the sustainable transformation of modern housing estates. She has written 10 recent peer-reviewed conference and journal articles relating to sustainable design and renovation for publications such as *Health Environments Research & Design* (HERD), DOCOMOMO and *Architectural Research Quarterly*. Her research expands the definition of sustainable architecture and the design of green buildings to encompass wellbeing and health with implications for research and practice.

Her current work engages with computation and new technologies, and intersections between sustainable design and health. Projects include utilising new technologies such as environmental, climatic and occupancy sensors and digital simulations to gain insights into experience and comfort and investigate architectural and behavioural conditions in interiors and exterior spaces. She is the co-editor of *Inside Smartgeometry: Expanding the Architectural Possibilities of Computational Design* (2013) and co-author of *Computing the Environment: Digital Design Tools for Simulation and Visualisation of Sustainable Architecture* (2017), both published by John Wiley & Sons.

With this title of △, she brings together her academic research, professional connections and publishing to explore the positive co-benefits of sustainable and healthy architecture in a range of settings. *Design for Health* examines emerging approaches in contemporary architectural practices relating to the conceptualisation and measurement of health and wellbeing in connection with changing notions of the environment.

Interconnected Approaches to Sustainable Architecture

INTRODUCTION

TERRI PETERS

Stantec and William McDonough + Partners,
UCSF Medical Center,
Mission Bay,
San Francisco,
2015

The interior of the University of California, San Francisco hospital was designed to focus on healthy materials and promote psychosocial health using strategies including daylight and views to the outdoors. Consultants McDonough Braungart Design Chemistry developed screening criteria for finishes and materials to minimise environmental toxins.

The challenges of integrating sustainable design into our buildings and cities, and improving our health and wellbeing, are interconnected. Our natural and built environments are an inextricable part of ourselves, and we influence – and are influenced by – a myriad of design decisions that impact the air we breathe, the water we drink, and the homes we live in. Priorities and design principles for concepts underlying sustainable design and health are culturally dependent and have changed dramatically over time, reflecting scientific knowledge, developments in building construction and architecture, and new trends and technologies for living and communicating with others. Health is tied to concepts of social connectedness, happiness and quality of life. This issue of △D thus explores a range of innovative design responses for health-promoting, sustainable architecture.

The World Health Organization (WHO) defines health as 'a state of complete physical, mental and social well-being and not merely the absence of disease or infirmity'.[1] The *Green Guide for Health Care*[2] defines the three key principles for healthy buildings as those that protect the immediate health of building occupants; the health of the local community; and the natural resources and health of the global community. The design details of therapeutic environments are culturally specific and depend on many factors, but essentially they need to support clinical excellence in the treatment of the physical body; support the psychosocial and spiritual needs of patients and their families as well as staff; and produce measurable positive effects on patients' clinical outcomes and staff effectiveness.[3] These are all positive criteria, but architectural quality could be made even more explicit, for example relating to the building's form and relationship to site, regarding choice of materials and interior finishes, and with respect to connection to the natural world – all of which are integral to therapeutic design.

Expanding the Definition of Sustainable Design

The work featured in this issue expands the framework of sustainable architecture to include comfort, wellness, security and health, focusing on the positive co-benefits of sustainable design and wellbeing in hospitals and health environments. While these buildings represent an important opportunity to use architectural design to positively impact people's experiences and health outcomes, they also present particular challenges relating to environmental sustainability. For example, hospitals have an extremely high energy-use intensity due to specialist equipment and 24-hour operation; they tend to occupy large footprints and are often designed as campuses taking up large blocks of centrally located land; and they have high operating costs, making them expensive to run and maintain. They have proven difficult to adapt for reuse once built, and the architectural quality is often questionable.

Healthcare facilities use a large proportion of our shared resources including energy, materials and land. These building types also benefit from a wealth of expert opinions and consultants including design programmers, planners and other healthcare design specialists who collaborate on the project. Yet still they could be much improved in terms of architectural design and patient experience. Additionally, the current trends of rebuilding and renovating modern healthcare facilities now need to consider demographic shifts such as an ageing population living longer than ever before, and designing 'future-proof' buildings that can adapt to new and emerging technologies. Global waves of renovation and rebuilding schemes are presenting unprecedented financial challenges as there is pressure to accommodate more patients, and to design to higher environmental standards. This *D* showcases high-quality architecture for health that aims to simultaneously achieve ambitious environmental, social and economic performance.

Throughout history, illness, and in particular communicable diseases, have plagued society, and this has been reflected in how we design for health. Today, however, it is non-communicable diseases such as heart attacks and strokes, cancer, chronic respiratory conditions and diabetes that present the greatest threats to life,[4] and depression is the leading cause of disability worldwide.[5] As buildings can influence our emotions and psychological wellbeing, they could therefore improve our mental health. How can good design and better connections to our environment enhance psychosocial health?

A look at recent and in-progress hospital projects reveals a variety of architectural approaches: some incorporating renewable energy and strategies for reducing carbon emissions; others testing ideas for integrating new technologies to better connect people with their health data and enable them to monitor the course of their care; as well as the siting of patient hotels and specialist clinics on local hospital campuses to improve community connectedness and encourage family support.

Ambitious Energy Performance and Patient-Oriented Care

Compared with innovations in 'low energy, low carbon' designs for other building types, there are relatively few environmentally sustainable hospital projects designed by high-profile architects. One pioneering example, however, is the new University of California, San Francisco (UCSF) Medical Center complex at Mission Bay in San Francisco (2015), designed by Stantec (formerly Anshen + Allen) and William McDonough + Partners as a health-promoting and architecturally innovative benchmark for sustainable architecture. Using half the energy of a typical hospital, its solar array aims to prevent 500 tonnes of carbon emissions yearly. Unique programmes for psychosocial health include facilities where children can make and record music or participate in broadcasts with other young patients in the hospital, and even continue school in a fully accredited classroom.[6] The project incorporates holistic sustainability principles such as maximising daylight, air quality and views outside; improving the natural habitat; designing for low emissions; expansive green roofs; strategies for water conservation; requirements for healthy materials; and offering educational and public services.

Another innovative project is the New Karolinska Solna University Hospital in Stockholm (due for completion in 2018), which illustrates global best practice in therapeutic hospital design. It will use about half the amount of energy as a typical hospital of this size, and will be certified using the Swedish third-party Miljobyggnad and LEED Gold. The aim of architects White Tengbom Team, a collaboration between two of Sweden's leading offices, is that 98 per cent of the building's energy needs will come from renewable sources including on-site geothermal. Temperature and air quality sensors will provide real-time feedback for environmental control systems. The interiors are based on the 'thematic care' concept where doctors and specialists visit the patients rather than the other way around. Natural light, integrated artwork, and connections to nature reflect the project's 'patients-first' approach. With high ceilings, robust joists, and the infrastructural and technical capacity to accommodate future needs, the architecture meets the requirement for a long-lasting building that can adapt over time.

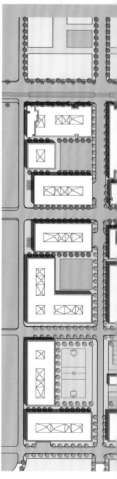

The project includes 1.6 hectares (4 acres) of green space including 0.4 hectares (1.2 acres) of rooftop gardens, many of which are designed as therapeutic spaces for adjacent patient care areas. Butterfly- and bird-friendly plantings were chosen in certain areas to give patients something beautiful to look at.

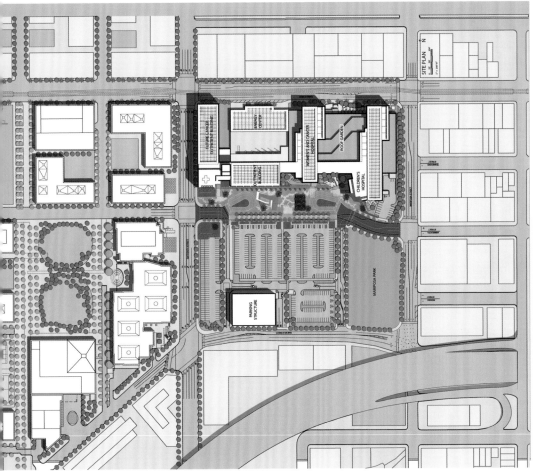

Twenty-four separate gardens and outdoor areas of respite are included in the hospital project. Derek Parker from the Center for Health Design contributed evidence-based design principles that included the provision of a variety of green spaces to promote health and wellbeing.

The single rooms

Throughout the NKS project, the planning and design of the new university hospital has been based on the needs of the patients. One central component is that all the hospital rooms are single rooms. In total, there are 630 single rooms, 28 in each ward, and they are 19 square metres.

Less spreading of infection
The fact that patients have their own hygiene rooms and there are fewer bed transports means the risk of infection spreading is reduced. The wash-basin in the single rooms also means care staff can wash their hands in close proximity to the patient.

Involvement
Patients have increased possibilities to be involved in their own care process and staff have more opportunities to adapt their care even further to the patients' needs.

Patient safety
The short distance between hospital bed and hygiene room reduces the risk of falls. The night light next to the hygiene room also improves patient safety since the patient can see where to walk in the night.

Design
The single rooms have an airy atmosphere and modern design. From the bed, patients can see out through the window and also adjust the blinds and control the TV. The end wall has a care panel and a cupboard for the patient's belongings.

Security and integrity
The patients can talk undisturbed with relatives and care staff. Relatives are also able to stay overnight in the room. The door leading into the room has a window so care staff can monitor the patient without unnecessary disturbance.

Choice of materials
The walls and ceiling are white with the exception of one feature wall which has a light shade of colour. The windows and care panels are framed with light wood. All the surface areas and materials are easy to keep clean.

Collaboration
Care staff can collaborate in work teams more easily and adapt their care to each individual patient. Collaboration between care, research and education is also facilitated.

Sustainability
Renewable electricity, resource-saving and environmentally-friendly materials, pleasant acoustic environment and presence-controlled lighting are examples of sustainable solutions in the single rooms which create an excellent indoor environment.

White Tengbom Team,
New Karolinska Solna
University Hospital,
Stockholm,
due for completion
2018

The entrance hall of the 730-bed facility will feature natural materials, energy-efficient LED lighting, and connections to the outdoors via skylights, windows and atriums.

Single rooms and private bathrooms for all patients have been proven to offer health benefits, in particular relating to the containment of infection. Single rooms also provide improved comfort, a sense of privacy and security. Each has a place for family to sit or sleep overnight.

New Communications Technologies

Advances in technologies for the design and operation of building systems as well as for record keeping and interactions with patients are changing the physical and social environments of hospitals. HOK's Humber River Hospital in Toronto (2015) is a 'fully digital hospital', where interactive technology allows for a new approach to resource use (less paper and paperwork), more space for patient care, and better communication between patients and staff. Each of the 650 patient rooms has a variety of digital screens: outside the door, on the wall and attached to the bed. Here, Wi-Fi can almost be considered a therapeutic amenity, providing ill and distressed patients with access to entertainment, communication with family, and information about their course of treatment from their bedside. The 'lean, green and digital' method employed in HOK's design aims to reduce energy use by 50 per cent of that of a typical facility, save more than $3 million a year in operating costs, offer better coordination between the hospital's different specialities and departments that support the various stages of patient care, including outpatient rehabilitation, and virtually engage with local community health partners beyond the hospital setting. It is hoped that these initiatives will contribute to the emotional and physical wellbeing of Humber River Hospital patients.

Emotionally Supportive Spaces

There is also a need for emotionally supportive environments on hospital campuses that provide care but are not clinical. Family-oriented spaces on hospital campuses such as those run by the Ronald McDonald House Charities (RMHC) provide short-term accommodation for families at little or sometimes no cost that allows them access to specialised medical treatment. The new Ronald McDonald House at BC Women's and Children's Hospital in Vancouver, designed by Michael Green Architects (MGA) in 2015, is a home-like setting where families can enjoy common spaces, kitchen and dining areas, fitness areas and library resources. It provides a healthy environment for children with compromised immune systems via daylighting, the use of natural materials throughout, and natural ventilation. It features an innovative tilt-up cross-laminated timber structure that is lightweight and environmentally friendly, a key strategy for the facility's expected LEED Gold rating. Though not a patient-care facility per se, MGA's focus on sustainable materials, architectural quality, and design for comfort and wellbeing nevertheless offers emotionally supportive and spiritual spaces for patients' families.

Architecture as Therapy

The essays in this issue address three broad, often interconnected themes: the potential of architecture to encourage a sense of wellbeing and offer therapeutic benefits; the need for multiple scales of integrated health-promoting interventions; and how salutogenic design can enhance sensory experiences for patients, visitors and staff. In each case, how the design of emotionally and physically supportive buildings can limit harm to their specific environments is also explored.

Charles Jencks writes about Maggie's Centres, an experimental programme of inspirational building projects spearheaded by Jencks and his late wife Margaret 'Maggie' Keswick Jencks in the late 1990s to provide supportive care for cancer patients through great architecture (see pp 66–75). The inspiring and provocative buildings, by high-profile designers, focus on wellbeing, the experience of nature and views outdoors, and fostering a sense of community.

In their essay 'Can Architecture Heal?' (pp 82–89), Michael Murphy and Jeffrey Mansfield of Mass Design Group connect to locally specific social and climatic conditions. The practice's recent projects include the Maternity Waiting Village in Malawi (2010), which aims to reduce maternal mortality rates by drawing on the principles of vernacular architecture to create highly desirable, comfortable and safe environments to care for expectant mothers.

Melbourne-based Lyons's daring and colourful attitude to healthcare architecture is illustrated in founding director Corbett Lyon's discussion (pp 56–65) of the evolution of the practice's thinking in creating new typologies for hospital design. Projects featured include the Lady Cilento Children's Hospital in South Brisbane, Queensland (2014). Comprehensible, manageable and meaningful, it was designed to reduce stress with features such as terraced roof gardens, bold exterior and interior colour and textures for wayfinding, and a high-performance bioclimatic facade.

Sunand Prasad's article on 'Regenerative Agents' (pp 122–7) describes Penoyre & Prasad's search for the architectural equivalent of 'patient-focused medicine'. The office's award-winning projects here outline three key strategies: creating flexible designs that can adapt to changing needs; connecting public and private spaces to produce a civic building 'of great social purpose'; and embodying regenerative, zero-waste and ecological design principles.

In 'Decoding Modern Hospitals' (pp 16–23), architect and architectural historian Annmarie Adams looks at how hospital design has transformed over the years in response to societal changes and architectural trends and movements. She concludes that hospitals should be both works of architecture, integrating novelty and inspiring design, as well as places for treatment.

Scales of Intervention

Multiple scales of intervention and a continuum of care are explored by designer Sylvia Leydecker (pp 76–81), who specialises in health-promoting interiors for emotional wellbeing. Her designs for a maternity unit and private patient rooms at a hospital in Germany use natural materials, daylight, colour and texture to create a sense of intimacy and comfort.

'In-between' spaces such as courtyards, porches and galleries are the focus of Terry Montgomery's contribution to the issue (pp 114–21). He argues that these threshold spaces can make or break a healthcare experience. Illustrated with recent projects by his practice Montgomery Sisam Architects, he reveals how the studio successfully elevates such spaces to a therapeutic role.

Salutogenic and Sensory Architecture

Julian Weyer's study (pp 32–41) of the healing environment at the CF Møller-designed Hospice Djursland in Rønde, Denmark (featured on the cover of this issue) has shown that the emphasis 'needs to be on the individual, his or her healing and access to daylight and green surroundings', as implied in the article's title: 'Lean, Green and Healthy'.

Advances in technologies are changing the physical and social environments of hospitals.

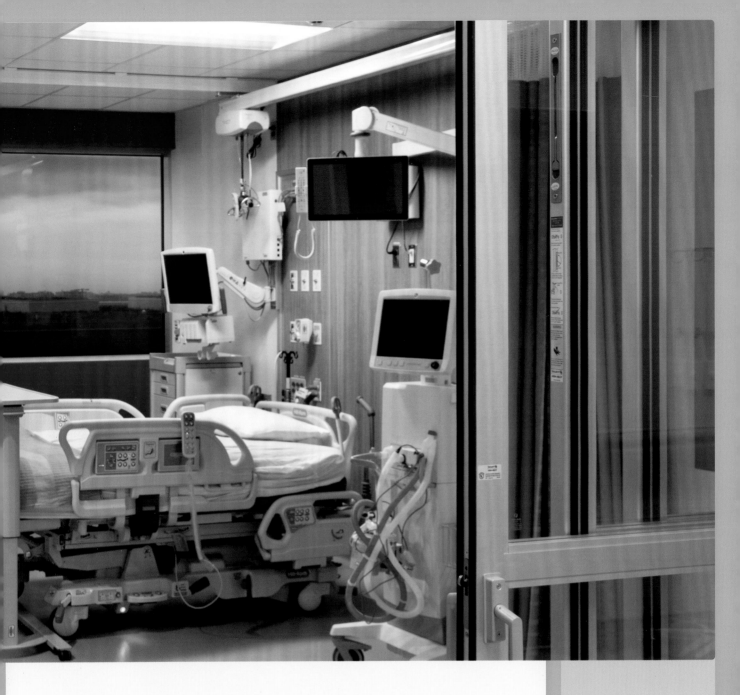

HOK,
Humber River Hospital,
Toronto,
2015

Each room has a display screen
at the entrance to display data
about the patient and their care,
such as allergies, risk of falls and
care updates. Inside the rooms,
every bed has its own computer
terminal so patients can access
their medical chart, adjust the
room lighting and temperature,
order meals, watch a movie and
use the Internet.

Architect Giuseppe Boscherini's 'A Sense of Coherence' (pp 108–13) begins with insights from his own patient experience, presenting a spatial framework for salutogenic design in his discussion of architecture and the senses. This theme is also picked up by Richard Mazuch of IBI Group (pp 42–7), who explores sense-sensitive healing environments as an aspect of therapeutic design.

Sensory design is explored in a different way by Sean Ahlquist, Leah Ketcheson and Costanza Colombi at the University of Michigan (pp 90–99), who illustrate a series of material and spatial installations as interactive environments for children with autism. The authors use their interdisciplinary collaboration and expertise in architecture, kinesiology and psychiatry to offer a rich theoretical discussion of designing for multisensory experience. They conclude that architecture can itself be a communicative device, and their approaches to customised metrics and therapeutic design propose new ways of thinking about social support and sustainability.

New Roles for Architects

The need for therapeutic and sustainable architecture can present new roles for designers, and not just in the field of healthcare facilities. Arup's Alisdair McGregor, Ann Marie Aguilar and Victoria Lockhart (pp 48–55) explore designing for health at the urban, neighbourhood, building and human scales in a variety of health-promoting, but not specifically healthcare,

Michael Green Architecture (MGA),
Ronald McDonald House,
Vancouver, Canada,
2014

above: The daylit interior is designed to be comfortable and relaxing with simple detailing and natural materials. Views to the outside offer places for people of all ages to play, dine and socialise in a home-like setting.

below: MGA used a prefabricated cross-laminated-timber structure with mass timber walls and a lightweight wood floor. This construction method was selected to enable it to transfer loads across open-plan areas to facilitate clear spaces at lower levels, creating a flexible interior that can be easily reorganised and adapted in future.

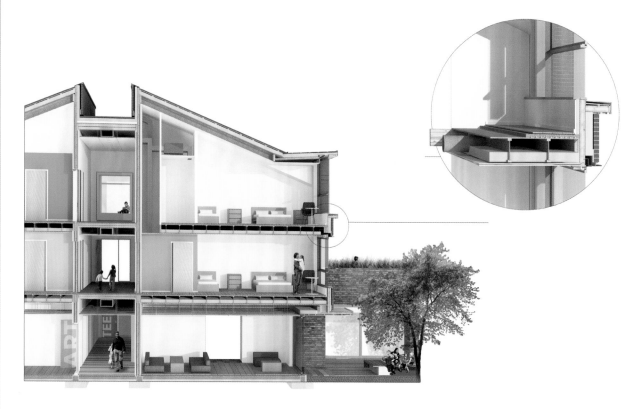

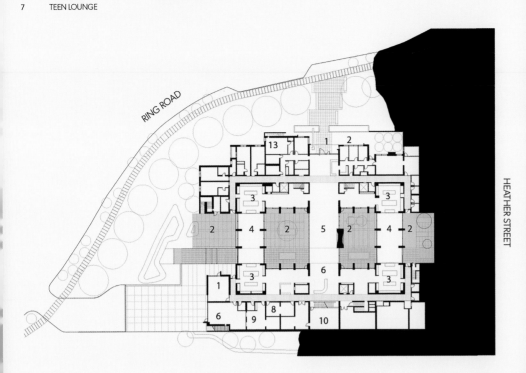

1	ENTRY	8	ARTS AND CRAFTS
2	COURTYARDS	9	FITNESS
3	KITCHEN	10	MULTI-PURPOSE
4	DINING	11	SUITE
5	LIVING ROOM	12	HOUSE LOUNGE
6	GAMES ROOM	13	MAGIC ROOM
7	TEEN LOUNGE		

RING ROAD

HEATHER STREET

Site plan. The design breaks down the 73-family facility into four 'houses' stitched together with common areas: dining rooms, living rooms and courtyards. The interiors are both restorative, and uncluttered and playful. Bright-yellow slides are a fun way for children to circulate in two-level play areas.

projects. They consider how architects might take an expanded role in designing for health, especially in light of new metrics for health and wellbeing such as the Well Building Standard.

In 'Architects as First Responders' (pp 100–107), Stephen Verderber explains how portable architecture for emergency and disaster relief can help communities bounce back, support their sustainability throughout the rebuilding process, and increase collective social capital in health-promoting ways.

More Ambitious Environmental Design

Design For Health: Sustainable Approaches to Therapeutic Architecture argues that definitions and metrics for sustainable design must be expanded to encompass and prioritise health and wellbeing, repositioning humans and human experience at its core. But there remain serious challenges for architects and designers in these areas. The positive co-benefits of sustainable design and human health are significant, and architects certainly have a role to play in the design of people's wellbeing, but they must take greater leadership in environmental design and sustainability. Examples have shown that barriers to more holistically sustainable healthcare designs are not merely technical, they are social and political, and designers need to find ways to better engage with these issues.

New technologies and ways of gathering and analysing site and climatic data could offer some opportunities; for example advances in digital tools for designing and constructing buildings could better enable collection and analysis of specific and relevant green buildings indicators. Such data might encompass quantitative building resource use, quality of experience, wellbeing, patterns of behaviour and occupation, which could support more effective and longer-lasting buildings and result in environments that can be more easily improved and retrofitted to help mitigate the financial and demographic challenges ahead. There is reason to be optimistic as architects continue to innovate and investigate the connections between patient experience, wellbeing and long-term thinking in healthcare design. ⌂

Notes
1. World Health Organization, Preamble to the Constitution of the World Health Organization as adopted by the International Health Conference, New York, 19–22 June 1946: www.who.int/about/definition/en/print.html.
2. A sustainable design toolkit organised by the non-profit organisations Health Care Without Harm and Centre for Maximum Potential Building Systems: see www.gghc.org/.
3. Ron Smith and Nicholas Watkins, 'Therapeutic Environments', Therapeutic Environments Forum, AIA Academy of Architecture for Health, 2010: www.wbdg.org/resources/therapeutic.php.
4. World Health Organization, 'Non Communicable Diseases', January 2015: www.who.int/mediacentre/factsheets/fs355/en/.
5. World Health Organization, 'Depression', April 2016: www.who.int/mediacentre/factsheets/fs369/en/.
6. Harvey M Bernstein, *The Drive Toward Healthier Buildings: The Market Drivers and Impacts of Building Design and Construction on Occupant Health, Well-being and Productivity*, McGraw Hill Construction (Bedford, MA), 2014, pp 32–3.

Decoding
Modern
Hospitals

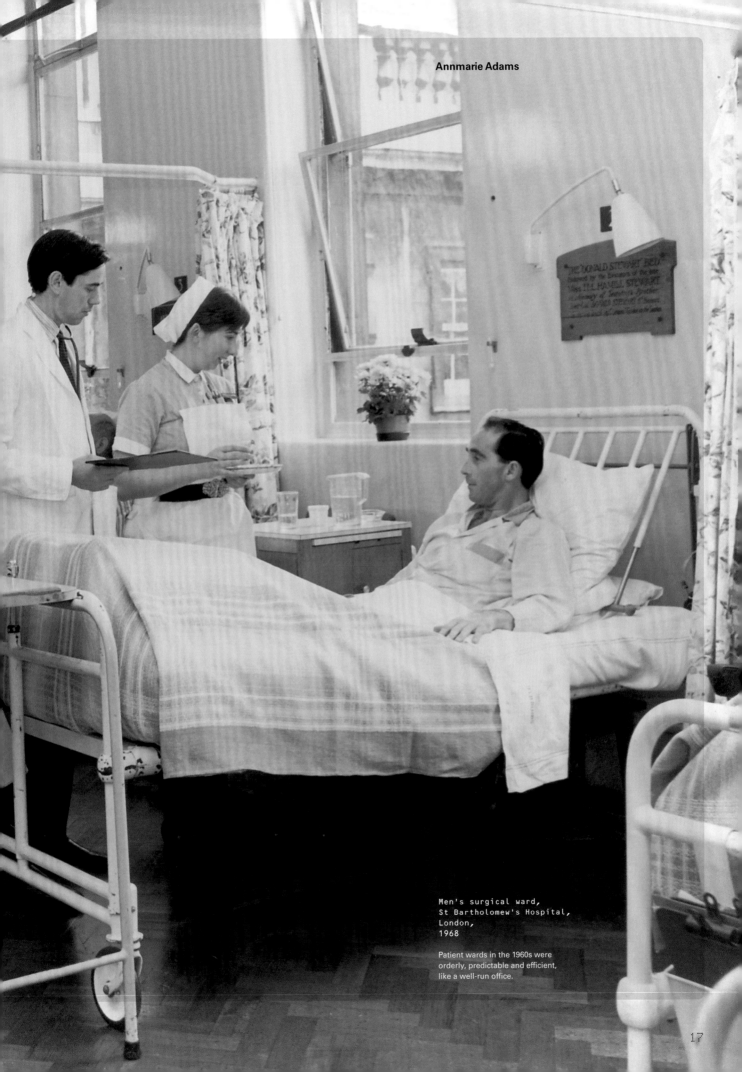

Annmarie Adams

Men's surgical ward,
St Bartholomew's Hospital,
London,
1968

Patient wards in the 1960s were
orderly, predictable and efficient,
like a well-run office.

The various currents in post-Second World War hospital architecture have shared one central aim: to 'normalise' the healthcare environment. Rather than looking obviously like hospitals, these buildings have gone from resembling office blocks, to shopping malls, to techno-utopias, to zoned campuses with a distinct local feel and a focus on sustainability. Professor **Annmarie Adams**, of Montreal's McGill University, refers to examples across North America and Europe to illustrate the different ways architects have found of putting the patient experience at the heart of their hospital design strategy.

Today's hospitals no longer look like hospitals. While the church has its steeple, the school has its playground and the hotel its lobby, the urban general hospital has only its size to announce itself. Except for the ubiquitous 'H' and emergency signage, a preponderance of ambulances, and perhaps a bunch of smokers with IVs, contemporary hospitals are often recognisable only by their magnitude. If anything, many new hospitals could pass as big-box stores or industrial parks. Like these corporate precedents, they are introverted, offering relatively little to their urban contexts. Bogged down by complex standards and stymied by pressures to justify design decisions through evidence-based research, ours is not the golden age of hospitals.

Hospital architecture was not always so inscrutable. Buildings from the 1950s and 1960s screamed out 'I'm a hospital'. These were looming towers on broad multistorey pads, with circular driveways and thousands of identical windows. A good example is Chicago's Mercy Hospital designed by CF Murphy in 1968. Such hospitals looked like office buildings, but conspicuously cheaper and a lot bigger. It is the hospital that many baby boomers picture from childhood, with elevators that 'ding' and open directly on to nurses' stations; straight, wide corridors with continuous wooden railings; and lobbies with a gift shop that sold hand-knitted baby things and Archie comics. Doctors in white coats populated these highly dignified, monochrome hospitals. Armed with stethoscopes and clipboards, they took charge and healed grateful patients through seemingly magical interventions like surgery and drugs. The architecture of the postwar hospital, through its association with the efficiency of modern business and its focus on heroic doctors, expressed the extraordinary power of medicine to cure.

CF Murphy,
Mercy Hospital,
Chicago, Illinois,
1968

The postwar tower hospital made older types instantly obsolete. Its clean, simple forms displaced the dark, intricate buildings of earlier generations.

Mall Hospitals

What do subsequent hospitals disclose about medicine? In the ensuing decades, their architectural message became much less clear, especially in North America. Whereas the baby-boomer hospital was efficiently arranged for physicians, for example, those designed for Generation X made it easy for patients and families. Rather than working towards a universal look, in the 1980s architects focused on making hospitals that would fit into their various communities. These were friendlier, accessible and, above all, 'less institutional'. They rejected the model of the office tower with identical floor plates and instead prescribed massive atriums that made hospitals appear less serious. Since libraries, museums and airports also donned atriums at this time, everything began to look like malls.

Part of the pitch for accessibility was what healthcare architecture specialist Professor Stephen Verderber calls 'horizontalism', where hospitals spread out across their sites and sometimes multiply, in lower-rise pavilions.[1] Colour also returned to the language of hospital design, and many projects in the 1980s included playful, almost whimsical colour combinations, inviting patients to de-stress upon entry. Concurrently, the spaces between hospital buildings became significant, giving rise to 'healing gardens' and other therapeutically charged landscapes.[2] Even the views from hospital windows could be deemed healthful. All these features – a campus-like plan, polychromy and links to nature – were intended to distract patients from the business of being seriously ill.

The mall hospital was the quintessential architecture of so-called 'patient-centred care', a movement that in the 1970s and 1980s saw patients become consumers, learn how to 'shop' for good healthcare and take charge of their own health decisions, and resulted in landmark documents such as the patient's bill of rights in the US.[3] Perhaps influenced by the hotel industry and parallel to broad trends towards privacy in the US, single rooms in hospitals became the norm during this period, with special accommodation that enabled family members to stay overnight – a concept unimaginable in postwar hospitals with their rigid visiting hours. Shorter and/or curving corridors, which unfolded like picturesque suburban crescents, and spa-inspired luxuries such as hot tubs and fitness rooms, gave certain hospitals a competitive edge. Children's hospitals even showcased lobbies with features commonly found at amusement parks, such as rides, making visits seem fun. Evelina London Children's Hospital designed by Hopkins Architects and completed in 2005 featured superheroes as window washers. Obstetric wards and birthing centres, in particular, drew on domestic references in an effort to demedicalise childbirth.[4] In all these ways, mall hospitals blurred the lines between healthcare, leisure and shopping in an effort to 'normalise' illness.

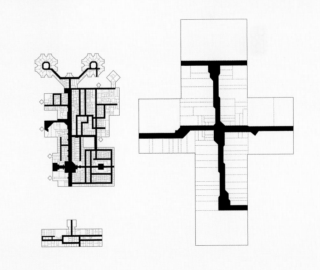

Shepley Bulfinch, Dartmouth–Hitchcock Medical Center, Lebanon, Grafton County, New Hampshire, 1991

Top: In the 1990s, inspiration from shopping malls made a trip to the hospital seem like an everyday event.

Above: Comparison of plans showing the significance of circulation in the mall and the hospital. Anchor retailers draw shoppers along a linear path, while patients follow a network configuration.

Zeidler Roberts Partnership Architects,
The Atrium,
Hospital for Sick Children (SickKids),
Toronto,
1993

above: Street lighting and artificial palm trees give the atrium lobby a semblance of exterior space.

below right: The cross-section of atrium hospitals, popular after the 1980s, facilitated wayfinding as visitors could see multiple levels at once.

Today mall hospitals seem somewhat conventional. The Dartmouth-Hitchcock Medical Center in Lebanon, New Hampshire, an early and influential 'mall' hospital designed by Shepley Bulfinch in 1991, has now been open a quarter of a century. In their book *Medicine Moves to the Mall* (2003), authors David C and Beverlie Conant Sloane explain how huge changes in American healthcare played out in hospital architecture, beginning with Medical City Dallas in 1974.[5] As they point out, the big idea behind Dartmouth-Hitchcock is not so much a city or an atrium, but a public circulation spine that offers retail, dining and everyday amenities to patients, staff and the wider community. It illustrates how late 20th-century hospitals truly use circulation as a driver, just like a mall. In malls or other spaces designed for consumption, visitors tend to walk slowly and don a relatively passive mode – a sort of 'mall crawl'. In this mode, urges hit consumers at will. In early mall hospitals, this same sense of relaxing ambulation is transferred to outpatient clinics, waiting areas and particularly lobbies, which were given ample square footage and became sites of intensive retail activity. Massive atrium lobbies such as the addition to the Hospital for Sick Children (also known as SickKids) in Toronto designed by Zeidler Roberts Partnership Architects (now Zeidler Partnership Architects) in 1993 is a good example.[6] Its familiar and open design invites Torontonians to visit – in stark contrast to the no-nonsense, austere hospital lobbies of the postwar decades.

In early mall hospitals, this same sense of relaxing ambulation is transferred to outpatient clinics, waiting areas and particularly lobbies

One advantage that hospitals of this period had over retail malls was their use of daylight and views as a wayfinding strategy and partner to medical treatment. Whereas in malls, disorientation can lead to spontaneous shopping, getting lost in hospitals can be problematic. In malls, consumers tend to walk from end to end, while hospital users always have a specific destination. Wayfinding in mall hospitals thus took its cues not from the retail mall, but from the ways people orient themselves in cities, through sight lines, zoning and memorable landmarks. Fountains, works of public art and other 'moments' designed into patient-centred hospitals helped patient-consumers find their way. This hospital-as-city metaphor was often explicit, with corridors even masquerading as streets, as if outside, with 'street' lighting and benches, giving the hospital an aura of being public, no matter what its pedigree. Massive skylights augmented the illusion that interior space was outside. Multistorey atriums meant users could see where they were going across levels, giving them an unprecedented sense of control.

Technology-Driven Hospital Design

While this projected image of normalcy pervaded hospital architecture of the late 20th century, it was sometimes just a veneer. Behind the cheery decoration, all of the necessary systems – computer, technical equipment and communications – handled the uncompromising demands of modern medicine. A significant architectural component in this 'backstage' architecture was the development of interstitial floors, where an entire level of the hospital was given over to mechanical equipment. Interstitial sections predate the mall hospital, having appeared at Louis Kahn's Salk Institute of Biological Studies in La Jolla, California, in 1966, and in Tufts Medical Center, Boston, Massachusetts, and the McMaster University Health Sciences Centre in Hamilton, Ontario, in 1972. Described by architectural theorist Reyner Banham as the 'ultimate medical megastructure',[7] McMaster occupies its own special category in hospital history. Designed by Craig, Zeidler and Strong (now Zeidler Partnership Architects) to be both big and visionary, it features a long-span space-frame structure with mobile units that could plug in, showing the world that the hospital could adapt and expand, driven by the ever-changing demands of modern medicine.

Craig, Zeidler and Strong,
McMaster University Health Sciences Centre,
Hamilton,
Ontario,
1972

This night-time photograph of the centre shows the hospital's infinitely expandable structural system, which offered unbounded potential for change.

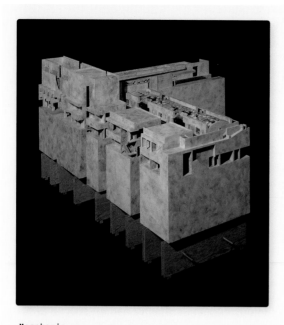

Morphosis,
Cedars-Sinai Comprehensive Cancer Center,
Los Angeles,
1988

Exceptional projects like this one avoided references
to the mall and faced the reality of serious illness.

Herzog & de Meuron,
New North Zealand Hospital,
Hillerød, Denmark,
2014

above: The organic footprint of this new hospital takes its cues from
nature. Shaped like a clover leaf and surrounded by a forest, the
horizontal scheme minimises distances between departments and
maximises patients' access to nature.

The dream of a techno-utopian hospital persists, however, in North America and Europe. The Hôpital Européen Georges-Pompidou in Paris, which opened in 2001, looks more like a city-within-a-city than a mall. Another striking example is Morphosis's Cedars-Sinai Comprehensive Cancer Center in Los Angeles (1988). In this now-demolished project, the architects tried to avoid what critic Paul Goldberger calls 'the soft, warm and cuddly' approach by confronting the tough, unsentimental reality of cancer.[8] Its innovation came from grouping all cancer protocols under one roof and from the use of a subterranean site. 'The project represented a profound exploration of architecture's potential for communicating compassion', claims the Morphosis website.[9]

Sustainable approaches to hospital design are producing interesting alternatives to the mall. An example is Herzog & de Meuron's 2014 design for the New North Zealand Hospital in Hillerød, Denmark. This 660-bed hospital, set in a Danish forest, is set to open in 2020. Its low-rise solution offers a distinctive spatial experience whereby all patient rooms are stacked on the perimeter of a subterranean base that houses two storeys of medical services. In the ways the building maximises air and light – all patient rooms have views of the forest – it looks back to the ubiquitous pavilion-plan hospital of the late 19th century. Its cross-section, however, is refreshingly novel. Engaging the site itself as inspiration for the design is an outward-looking alternative to the inward-looking mall plan. It is certainly no ordinary hospital.

Recoding Modern Hospitals

Making hospitals that looked like office towers or shopping malls succeeded in shifting expectations about illness and medicine. The point of those buildings was to make visiting them seem normal. However, today people expect more from hospitals. With the belief that good hospital design should inspire wellness, architecture has taken on a new role as part of the toolkit that makes patients better. But improving hospital architecture requires fresh perspectives. When firms that do not necessarily specialise in healthcare design major hospitals, the results are often imaginative. Healthcare architecture advances when architects embrace medical technology and landscape as inspiration, rather than as constraints or things to be disguised. Despite the benefits of the consumer turn in healthcare, illness is still a very serious subject. Healthcare thus deserves dignified buildings, inspired by the world around us. ᗪ

below: Every patient room in the design for this large hospital, which is due to open in 2020, has a view of the surrounding forest.

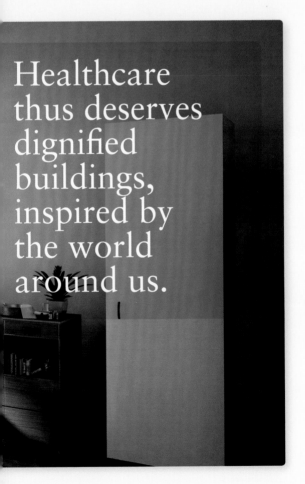

Healthcare thus deserves dignified buildings, inspired by the world around us.

Notes
1. Stephen Verderber and David J Fine, *Healthcare Architecture in an Era of Radical Transformation*, Yale University Press (New Haven, CT), 2000, p 201. See also Verderber's article on pp 100–107 of this issue of ᗪ.
2. Deborah Franklin, 'How Hospital Gardens Help Patients Heal', *Scientific American*, 1 March 2012: www.scientificamerican.com/article/nature-that-nurtures/.
3. Nancy Tomes, *Remaking the American Patient*, UNC Press (Chapel Hill, NC), 2016.
4. Ian Forbes et al, 'Birthing Unit Design: Researching New Principles', *World Health Design*, October 2008: www.worldhealthdesign.com/birthing-unit-design-researching-new-principles.aspx.
5. David C Sloane and Beverlie Conant Sloane, *Medicine Moves to the Mall*, Johns Hopkins University Press (Baltimore, MD), 2002, p 110.
6. See Annmarie Adams et al, 'Kids in the Atrium: Comparing Architectural Intentions and Children's Experience in a Pediatric Hospital Lobby', *Social Science & Medicine*, 70, 2010, pp 658–67.
7. Reyner Banham, *Megastructures: Urban Futures of the Recent Past*, Harper & Row (New York), 1976, p 139.
8. Paul Goldberger, 'ARCHITECTURE VIEW: A Tough Building Helps Patients Fight Disease', *The New York Times*, 24 February 1991: www.nytimes.com/1991/02/24/arts/architecture-view-a-tough-building-helps-patients-fight-disease.html.
9. Morphosis, 'Cedars-Sinai Comprehensive Cancer Center': www.morphosis.com/architecture/31/.

Super_archi-tecture

Terri Peters

SLA,
Climate adaptation
proposals for
Hans Tavsens Park
and Korsgade,
Copenhagen,
2016–

Korsgade road provides a green route through the city with connected spaces. Hans Tavsens Park will act as a rainwater catchment basin during cloudbursts, and then the excess rainwater will be led via Korsgade out into Peblinge Lake, being biologically purified on the way by the city park greenery on Korsgade.

Building for Better Health

Is minimising the negative effects of human activity on people and the planet enough, or can we aim even higher? Guest-Editor **Terri Peters** introduces the concept of superarchitecture: architecture that is not merely sustainable, but offers positive benefits for both human wellbeing and the environment. As demonstrated by the three international case studies she presents, it is applicable not only to healthcare architecture, but also to the spaces in which we live and work, and the wider urban realm. At its heart is a deep connection with nature.

Our attitudes to human health and the natural world have changed over time, and this has shaped our buildings and cities. We have long known that local climate and qualities of water, air, trees and soil impact human health, and there have been many different architectural responses. The idea of intense exposure to nature as a cure for illness found built form in many countries from about 1885 to 1950 in response to the tuberculosis crisis. Fresh-air treatments sparked new healthcare typologies, like sanatoria (a notable example being Alvar Aalto's Paimio Sanatorium, built in 1933 – see p 59) and cure cottages (such as those at Saranac Lake in New York starting from the 1870s), as well as therapeutic architectural features such as roof decks and cure porches.

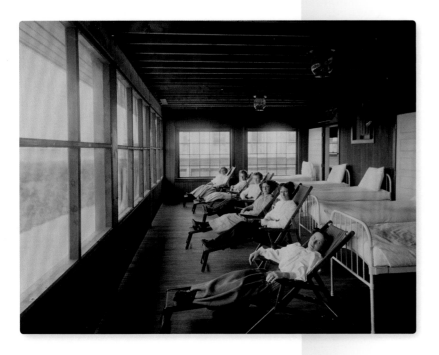

During this time there was a renewed interest in public health and living spaces, and many theories and guidelines were developed about design and wellbeing. In the 1910s Thomas Spees Carrington, an American medical doctor and prolific writer on sanatorium construction and also on do-it-yourself approaches for adapting fresh-air treatments at home, offered medical advice, drawings and photographs of how to use nature to improve health.[1] He explained methods for installing cure porches, creating pop-up tent shelters on shared apartment roofs, and using temporary window tents to funnel air from the window into the bed. He even advised on the use of 'knitted helmets' for sleeping that cover the entire face except the nostrils to protect from draughts. Spatial and material interventions allowed people to be exposed to nature's medicinal properties, to treat illness and to prevent it as well.

Ninette Sanatorium, Manitoba, Canada, c 1910

Women patients taking the cure in the sleeping pavilion. Cure porches offered a fresh-air cure and, combined with a relaxing natural setting and good nutrition, were leading approaches to tuberculosis treatment until the advent of antibiotics.

Regreening for Wellbeing

People still believe in the benefits of intense exposure to nature. Increasingly, however, the quality of climate matters: not only on a local and observable level, but also – due to awareness about climate change – on a global level, which is more abstract and difficult to quantify. With more than half the world now living in cities, research has shown that urban environments can negatively impact mental health,[2] so incorporating natural elements such as trees, air, light and water into the city is growing ever more important. Researchers have analysed the myriad of positive health benefits of green spaces, and even small doses of green, or 'vitamin G', has been proven to have lasting physical and mental health benefits.[3] For example, planting trees in an urban environment, aside from mitigating urban heat island effect, removing carbon dioxide from the air, storing carbon, and releasing oxygen into the atmosphere, can make people feel younger and richer. Findings published in the journal *Nature* showed that planting trees, even only ten on a city block, improves health perception in residents in ways comparable to adding $10,000 to their personal salaries, and being seven years younger.[4] Trees also offer design benefits including beauty, privacy, reduction of glare and reflection, buffering noise and creating comfort through shading. Part of an increasing interest in environment-health research made famous by Roger Ulrich's benchmark study in 1984 showing people healing faster when their hospital beds have views of nature,[5] a new industry, and renewed urgency, was strengthened around design and public health – not just for healthcare settings but all around us; and architecture and urban design could be at the centre of it.

Future Buildings Must Be Superarchitecture

Superarchitecture is a concept introduced here as designs that do more than minimise harm, a special category of buildings that offer measurable and integrated positive co-benefits for environmental sustainability and human health and wellbeing. This way of conceptualising healthy and green buildings argues that designers should strive for ways that the right environment can not only improve recovery, but also, in proper doses, can augment our physical and mental faculties, and make us even better than we were before. Daylight, airflow, thermal comfort, spatial variation, access to nature, building details, furniture and fittings, colour schemes and even acoustic qualities should be considered in the architectural design of sustainable buildings. Studies have shown that buildings with high-performing environmental design offer benefits for health and wellbeing.[6]

In the future, with increased focus on cities, resources, public health and shifting demographics, there will be a great need for Superarchitecture, for green/health infrastructure and building strategies that work at multiple scales, as multifunctional strategies for our physical environment and improving health. The examples of this new green typology are identified here based on their design intentions to impact a myriad of wellbeing and ecological systems. The three examples discussed in this essay are not healthcare facilities, but there are clear implications for care environments. They offer demonstrations of process-driven approaches to connecting to neighbourhood-scale climate-change adaptation in cities; net zero energy and water in office buildings to contribute to worker productivity and wellness; reconsidering the design of residences using digital simulation to achieve ambitious daylight factor levels; and utilising new building control technologies to offer more therapeutic and comfortable spaces for living.

The Extra Benefits of Climate Adaptation

Retrofitting urban areas to reflect the realities of climate change and extreme weather are high priorities for health and urban design. Research has found at least 11 complex and urgent health research areas related to climate change, including asthma and respiratory allergies, foodborne diseases and nutrition, and mental health- and stress-related disorders.[7] In response to research of this kind, new integrated urban design and climate adaptation projects are being designed and built in Copenhagen. One of the first of many such projects for the Danish capital is multidisciplinary practice SLA's scheme for Hans Tavsens Park and Korsgade, due for completion in 2018. The proposal integrates water features such as 'smart cloudburst solutions',[8] paving patterns, vegetation, irrigation and active design principles, both in the renewed Hans Tavsens Park and in a multifunctional and creative new streetscape and route along the main road of Korsgade.

SLA,
Climate adaptation proposals for Hans Tavsens Park and Korsgade, Copenhagen, 2016–

below & below middle:
The integrated climate adaptation and urban design proposals by SLA offer new activities, routes and environments for people as well as strategies for stormwater management, water purification, and 'cloudburst' roads.

It can be considered Superarchitecture as it goes beyond mitigating the impacts of climate change and integrates bike routes and walkways, offers new spatial experiences by designing with water and vegetation, and offers community benefit through opportunities to garden and tend to nature and new amenity spaces. Importantly it is also linked up through the Korsgade road, which connects the interventions from the city square to the water's edge. The project is designed for climate adaptation, but designer Stig L Andersson argues it offers intangible architectural quality, the 'extra benefits we get from climate adaptation: The blue, the green, the health, the active and the social. In short: All what [sic] makes life in the city worth living.'[9]

In 2015 the City of Copenhagen announced plans for 300 integrated climate adaptation and urban design interventions for Copenhagen. SLA won the Nordic Built Challenge Competition for their proposals for Hans Tavsens Park and Korsgade, which build on existing urban paths and offer new experiences with health and environmental benefits.

Biophilic Design for Natural Ecosystems and Human Wellbeing

The concept of biophilia offers relatively untapped potentials for green buildings generally, but also for Superarchitecture. Biophilia has been defined as the urge to affiliate with other forms of life,[10] and in design this means designing with nature and human wellbeing in mind. Eight points of the biophilic effect have been identified – light, colour, gravity, fractals, curves, detail, water and life – and these have been expanded with architecturally relevant concepts as a framework for exploring how designers could create health-promoting buildings.[11] However, there are few biophilia examples that are benchmarks for both environmental sustainability and design quality.

The Bullitt Center is a pioneering office building in Seattle by Miller Hull Partnership built in 2013. The client is the Bullitt Foundation, a non-profit group that focuses on urban ecology. The project was designed to be a living laboratory and 'the greenest commercial building in the world', with a designed lifespan of 250 years. In 2015 after a series of post-occupancy evaluations, it was certified according to the rigorous sustainability requirements of the Living Building Challenge Standard 2.1, which required that the building be net zero energy, net zero water, use non-toxic materials, provide a net increase of functional ecosystem area, enhance human health, contribute to social equity, and emphasise beauty.[12] It generates more energy than it needs, and an online real-time dashboard shows its resource use and how much it is giving back to the community.[13]

Miller Hull Partnership, Bullitt Center, Seattle, Washington, 2013

The Bullitt Center was designed to meet the Living Building Challenge metrics and studies were carried out relating to ecosystems services. Seven 'petals' identify strategies for equity, beauty, materials, site, water, energy and health.

Daylight and Wellness

Daylight is an experiential quality closely linked to architectural effect, energy savings and health promotion. As in the examples of sanatorium design and in contemporary hospital environments, exposure to daylight has been linked to positive health outcomes such as reduced length of stay, decreased medication intake and positive moods.[14] Researchers examining workplace productivity have found daylight can promote higher performance, reduce absenteeism, lower employee turnover and offer financial savings.[15] In all contexts daylight has been linked to nervous and endocrine systems, circadian cycles and other health aspects, and in schools it is linked to better attendance and higher achievements. Researchers often study the benefits of daylight and views outdoors together, because of the obvious links and co-benefits.

The Active House at Centennial Park, Toronto (2016) is one in a series of demonstration houses in the Velux® model homes series. Designed by Toronto-based architecture practice superkül, it focuses on natural daylight and ventilation for optimal indoor environmental qualities for sustainability and wellbeing, and it is designed in accordance with Active House principles, set out by the non-profit organisation Active House Alliance. The house has operable triple-paned windows and programmable skylights, as well as a TESLA® POWERWALL® rechargeable lithium-ion battery system for the home that pulls electricity from its energy provider (in this case a provider whose grid is 100 per cent renewable) during off-peak hours. After it was

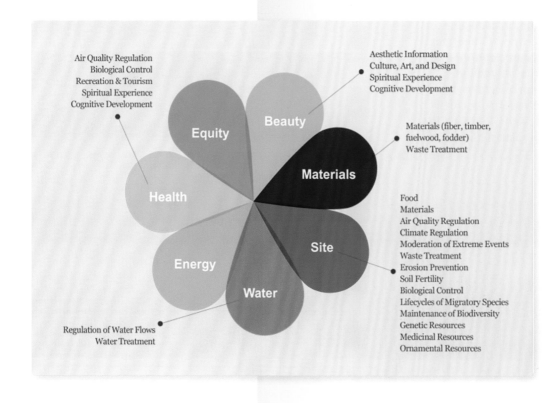

Air Quality Regulation
Biological Control
Recreation & Tourism
Spiritual Experience
Cognitive Development

Aesthetic Information
Culture, Art, and Design
Spiritual Experience
Cognitive Development

Materials (fiber, timber, fuelwood, fodder)
Waste Treatment

Food
Materials
Air Quality Regulation
Climate Regulation
Moderation of Extreme Events
Waste Treatment
Erosion Prevention
Soil Fertility
Biological Control
Lifecycles of Migratory Species
Maintenance of Biodiversity
Genetic Resources
Medicinal Resources
Ornamental Resources

Regulation of Water Flows
Water Treatment

Equity
Beauty
Materials
Health
Site
Energy
Water

superkül,
Active House,
Centennial Park,
Toronto,
2016

The Active House at
Centennial Park has an
average daylight factor
of 3.3 per cent (much
higher than the typical
2 per cent), triple-glazed
windows and skylights.

superkül,
Active House,
Centennial Park,
Toronto,
2016

Floorplans showing
daylight simulation.

Ground Floor

Second Floor

Daylight Factor %
10.0
8.8
7.8
6.8
5.5
4.4
3.2
2.0

The house is the world's
first Active House certified
residence. Active House
specifications consider
the site location, climate,
life-cycle costs, thermal
comfort, indoor air quality
and energy sources.

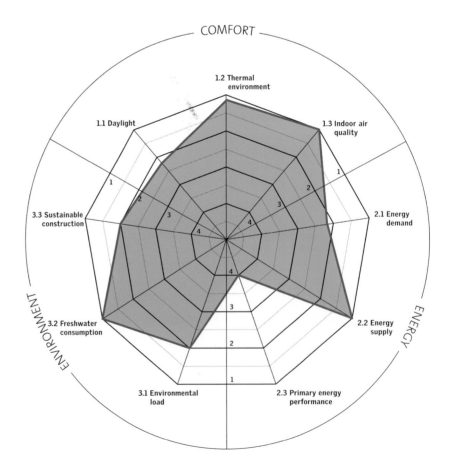

completed in 2016, a Velux employee and his family moved into the house to document their experiences and blog about how it feels to live there, describing its psychological impact on their comfort and wellbeing as well as how easy the technologies for operating the house are to use.[16]

Superarchitecture: Design as Therapy

This discussion of Superarchitecture has highlighted some ways designers are reconceptualising buildings and sites as potentially having therapeutic and environmental benefits, not just minimising resource use and meeting minimum standards. As discussed, landscape and urban-scale interventions are capable of doing more than reducing harm: planting trees could actually help us feel younger and richer while simultaneously cleaning our air and shading our sidewalks; and redesigning public squares to incorporate green infrastructure and encourage physical activity can be part of an integrated approach to adapting the built environment for extreme weather and climate change. The building-scale examples show how a workplace can offer biophilic benefits by better connecting us to other living things including our coworkers in a design that encourages social interaction, while generating surplus energy and water to benefit the community; and how a home designed to maximise daylight, natural ventilation and comfort can respond to the need and behaviours of inhabitants while also generating more energy than it needs.

In keeping with new studies of regenerative design, or ways that the act of building can be a catalyst for positive change within the unique place,[17] Superarchitecture attempts to re-frame discussions of environment and health with a focus on architectural design and quality. More work is needed in terms of framing a critical discussion about nature and its varied qualities and local meanings. Like health and architecture, people's attitude to nature is complex and culturally dependent, and while Carrington viewed nature fairly uncritically, as almost everything out-of-doors, we need to take a more critical and nuanced view of concepts of environment and nature, as we design for the next generations of inhabitants in our cities and communities. ⌂

Notes

1. Thomas Spees Carrington, *Directions for Living and Sleeping in the Open Air*, The National Association for the Study and Prevention of Tuberculosis (New York), 1910.
2. Florian Lederbogen et al, 'City Living and Urban Upbringing Affect Neural Social Stress Processing in Humans', *Nature*, 474(7352), 2011, pp 498–501.
3. Frances E (Ming) Kuo, *Parks and Other Green Environments: Essential Components of a Healthy Human Habitat*, National Recreation and Park Association (Ashburn, VA), 2010.
4. Omid Kardan et al, 'Neighborhood Greenspace and Health in a Large Urban Center', *Nature: Scientific Report 5*, article 11610, 2015, pp 1–13.
5. Roger S Ulrich, 'View Through a Window May Influence Recovery from Surgery', *Science*, 27 April 1984, 224(4647), pp 420–21.
6. There are many studies in a range of disciplines that show that green buildings have positive health impacts including: Magali A Delmas and Sanja Pekovic, 'Environmental Standards and Labor Productivity: Understanding the Mechanisms that Sustain Sustainability, *Journal of Organizational Behavior* 34, 2013, pp 230–52; Norm G Miller, Dave Pogue, Quiana D Gough and Susan M Davis, (2009). 'Green Buildings and Productivity', *Journal of Sustainable Real Estate*, 1(1), pp 65–89; and A Singh, M Syal, SC Grady and S Korkmaz, 'Effects of Green Buildings on Employee Health and Productivity', *American Journal of Public Health*, 100(9), 2010, pp 1665–8.
7. Christopher J Portier et al, *A Human Health Perspective On Climate Change: A Report Outlining the Research Needs on the Human Health Effects of Climate Change*, Environmental Health Perspectives / National Institute of Environmental Health Sciences (Research Triangle Park, NC), 2010.
8. For more on Copenhagen's 'cloudburst roads', see *Klimakvarter: Teknik- og Miljøforvaltningen Byens Fysik [Climate Neighbourhoods: Technical and Environmental Department of Urban Physics]*, http://klimakvarter.dk/en/skybrudsveje/.
9. SLA, Bryggervangen Skt Kjelds, 2016, http://www.sla.dk/en/projects/bryggervangen-sktkjelds
10. Edward O Wilson, *Biophilia*, Harvard University Press (Cambridge, MA), 1984.
11. Nikos A Salingaros, *Biophilia and Healing Environments: Healthy Principles For Designing the Built World*, Terrapin Bright Green (New York), 2015.
12. The Living Building Challenge is the most rigorous green building certification programme, created in 2006 by the International Living Future Institute: http://living-future.org/lbc.
13. The building dashboard for the Bullitt Center is online at http://buildingdashboard.com/clients/bullittcenter/ and shows the buildings energy generation and use in real time. It also shows other parameters such as water use, cistern levels, and local weather.
14. Agnes E van den Berg, 'Health Impacts of Healing Environments: a Review of Evidence for Benefits of Nature, Daylight, Fresh Air, and Quiet in Healthcare Settings', dissertation, Wageningen University and Research Center, Wageningen, The Netherlands, 2005, http://www.agnesvandenberg.nl/healingenvironments.pdf.
15. Canada Green Building Council, *Healthier Buildings in Canada 2016: Transforming Building Design and Construction* (Ottawa), 2016.
16. The blog by the inhabitants of the Centennial Park Active House in Toronto: http://greatgulf.com/activehouse/.
17. Raymond J Cole, 'Transitioning from Green To Regenerative Design', *Building Research and Information*, 40(1), 2012, pp 39–53.

Julian Weyer

Lean, Green and Healthy

Landscape and Health

The Scandinavian firm CF Møller has been designing healthcare buildings to high acclaim since 1931. Guided by humanistic values from the outset, they have developed three design principles that they apply to every commission, to favour patients' empowerment in the healing process. **Julian Weyer**, one of the practice's current partners, sets out these principles and explains how they have shaped several of their recent projects in Denmark: from a rural hospice, to a city-integrated care centre, to the country's largest hospital, town-like in scale and arrangement.

CF Møller Architects
with CF Møller Landscape,
Hospice Djursland,
Rønde,
Denmark,
2007 and 2011

As a demonstration project, the Hospice Djursland introduced the use of architecture, art and nature as integrated aspects of palliative treatment, defining a new kind of welfare architecture that seeks to reconcile patients with the prospect of death.

Our life starts with an inhalation and ends with an exhalation, and there is great human significance in this fact. For most of us these two unavoidable and ultimate phases of life will be in clinical environments – with clinical care.

Designing for today's healthcare should start with the end in mind: nature and proximity. These are what matter during the final days before a life ends. A recent hospice design by CF Møller, Hospice Djursland in Rønde, Denmark (built in two phases, 2007 and 2011) was the setting for a research study into patient experience and wellbeing. At a time when everything is counted, measured and weighed – numbers of patients, days in hospital, numbers of deaths and numbers discharged – this study sought to quantify something that is not normally assessed in this way: quality of life at a hospice.

Through a camera lens, patients and relatives captured everyday experiences, events and routines during the days before they died. Researchers used ZMET (Zaltman metaphor elicitation technique) – a patented qualitative research technique – with patients and their families being provided with a camera and asked to photograph what affects their daily lives in a hospice. The result was the book entitled *Det som har betydning* (meaning *What Really Matters*) – a touching and honest documentation of life lived, against all odds, at a hospice. A life that, at Hospice Djursland, must still be found worth living.

One patient documented in the book – Lise, aged 39 – reflected on her experience over two months at the hospice in 2012. Her words can be translated as:

> This is the best view in Denmark, with the light changing constantly, and you can see far into the distance. This gives a sense of peace and has a therapeutic effect. You can let your thoughts wander, and think about anything at all, because there is space for it – plenty of space. The beauty makes me want to be here. When I sit and enjoy nature, I can switch off the cognitive part of my brain and just meditate. Nature is important to me.[1]

Nature and the proximity between patients, personnel and relatives are important everyday resources during a difficult time. At Hospice Djursland, the landscape is not an option, but an embracing physical backdrop that is always present. The hospice is a fine example of how the deliberate fusion of building and landscape can draw in the landscape as a recurring, proximate physical backdrop for meeting other people, meeting oneself, and meeting death.

Hospice Djursland is first and foremost a building within a landscape. No matter where you go in the building – the reception area, the garden of the senses, the orangery, the atriums, the staff room, the lounge, the reflection room or the patient rooms – the beautiful landscape is always present.

Landscape and Urbanism as Design Drivers

Hospice Djursland was a pioneering demonstration project of the potential of integrating building and landscape in the healthcare sector. A rapidly increasing number of research reports and scientific studies provide evidence for the beneficial health aspects of good architecture and attractive environments, such as the importance of daylight for physical and psychological wellbeing, motivation and performance.[2] Accordingly, CF Møller engages with these issues during the design of health projects. The first hospital design by the firm in 1931 already clearly embodied this, and the practice continues to work with a blend of evidence- but also experience-based design that reflects the humanistic values of the Scandinavian modern movement.

Integrating healthcare architecture with landscape, being able to see and use green settings, also has a positive impact on people's physical and mental wellbeing in hospitals, homes and workplaces. A number of surveys point to landscapes and gardens as a significant free space for all users of hospitals, whether they are patients, staff or next-of-kin, which can help to reduce stress and play a key role for both social relations and individual privacy.[3]

At CF Møller, the potential of public space and landscape is seen as far more than self-evident added quality to the built environment or a consolation for users in difficult circumstances. One of the distinguishing marks of the firm's healthcare design process is blending urban design, landscape, building design and building component design. Rather than something to be filled in between buildings, landscape and urbanism are often the tools used initially which in turn become the very structure that makes especially large-scale institutions navigable and comprehensible.

Current trends mean that hospitals in general are undergoing a transformation. From being based on and serving one individual region, they are fast becoming part of an overall national and international strategy. In other words, hospitals in Scandinavia are decreasing in number but increasing in size. The need to gather all specialised fields at the large trauma centres and emergency hospitals has naturally led to large, cohesive structures that are not necessarily very clear and transparent. Technological developments and equipment-related challenges have contributed to accelerating this development. Complicated and expensive investments in medico-technical equipment lead to a natural centralisation of treatment, together with the need for integrated research and training facilities. This in turn leads to very large, complex hospital structures with administrative and operational rationales requiring a robust overall strategy to afford the structure evidence-based values – values reflecting how individual patients and members of staff perceive and are influenced by their physical surroundings.

Efficiency Through Architectural Quality

As a result, design must focus on therapeutic qualities that accelerate the patient's healing process and ensure a working environment with reduced errors and stress. This approach of putting the 'patient at the centre', rather than just making it an efficient place to work, is based on privileging the individual's perceptive experience of the health environment, and is a key supplement to the conventional requirements of functionality, logistics and optimisation of operations.

The CF Møller team has found that focusing on urbanistic and landscape design principles is the most effective way to provide this integration and a simple and secure wayfinding strategy, since another key aspect is the ability to read and understand one's surroundings. A well-functioning layout and infrastructure to promote easy navigation in buildings and indeed throughout the site is a fundamental prerequisite for a hospital to function optimally, as the special circumstances of a hospital visit may lead to higher stress levels that not only diminish users' ability to understand and process information, but also inhibit the body's self-curing capacities. In every possible way, users must be given a sense of being in control, as a key factor in reducing stress, anxiety and fear.

Focus on the patient means that the perception of large, rational structures is broken down into a number of recognisable and familiar spatial flows. And with this reference to the familiar framework of everyday life, the building complex becomes an allegory of the surrounding city's familiar framework.

CF Møller has developed three design principles of therapeutic empowerment: wayfinding, daylighting, and access to landscape. These form the basic DNA of projects such as the award-winning Akershus University Hospital in Oslo (2015), and current designs such as the New University Hospital in Aarhus, Denmark (begun in 2007 and due for completion in 2019).

The role of the hospital is changing from a place of (reactive) treatment to a place of (proactive) prevention, which makes the urban integration of the hospital even more important. At CF Møller, the aim is to make hospitals places where healthy people will also want to come, so included in the designs are community amenities such as spaces for fitness, rehabilitation, health talks, self-check workshops and children's learning facilities. These are integrated into the immediate surroundings, reconnecting the often-isolated healthcare complexes to the city and society.

In the Image of the City

The New University Hospital in Aarhus is part of a major redesign of the entire Danish healthcare sector. It is the first of a new series of so-called 'superhospitals' under construction, which will accommodate the highest levels of specialised treatments, including further CF Møller designs such as the Køge University Hospital (begun 2015, due for completion 2021).

For new large-scale projects like the New University Hospital in Aarhus, the design must create a hospital that on the one hand has a highly efficient layout, and on the other is perceived as a friendly and informal place. The design combines a safe and small-scale patient environment that encourages a fast recovery, together with an efficient working environment that is supported by integrated technology in order to allow the staff to remain close to patients. These design decisions form the basis of the salutogenic concept, which includes the implementation of general design principles such as the exclusive use of single-bed wards in small, intimate clusters, and a strong symbiosis between architecture and landscape design, ensuring views and access to green landscapes.

An existing university hospital (also designed by CF Møller in the 1980s) is an integral part of the new complex, thus augmenting its size from around

CF Møller Architects with Schønherr Landscape and Bjørbekk & Lindheim, Akershus University Hospital, Oslo, 2015

A glass-covered inner main street, in which wood is the dominating material, links the various buildings and functions and reveals the influence of the high priority given to easy wayfinding, daylight for all workplaces, views of the surrounding landscape, and contact with the outside environment.

CF Møller Architects with Cubo Arkitekter, Schønherr Landscape and DNU Consultancy Group, New University Hospital in Aarhus, Denmark, 2007–

above left: The biggest hospital construction project in Danish history, the New University Hospital in Aarhus is built onto the existing Aarhus University Hospital, in the Skejby neighbourhood, to form a combined hospital complex of almost 400,000 square metres (4.3 million square feet).

above: The large hospital complex project is pioneering in the development of 'healing architecture' in the Danish health sector and is organised like a town, with a hierarchy of neighbourhoods, streets and squares, enabling intuitive wayfinding.

150,000 square metres (1.6 million square feet) to almost 400,000 square metres (4.3 million square feet). Since the existing hospital is regularly voted Denmark's best hospital, a key challenge has been to achieve the increase in scale without compromising the desirable qualities and positive user experience of the existing low-rise layout. In particular the existing hospital is easily navigable and has decentralised patient access, and the setting is green and informal.

CF Møller's approach to the renovation and extension is to organise the New University Hospital complex like a town, creating easily recognisable blocks within a hierarchy of neighbourhoods, and designing streets and squares as a strategy to enable intuitive wayfinding by the users. The decentralised layout is made even more practical by a new ring road surrounding the entire complex, giving all users direct access to the individual treatment clusters, which all remain close to the ground in line with the quality of the existing hospital. At the heart of the entire complex is a large green park, alongside which the main circulation connects the treatment clusters and vertical accesses to bed wards – thus enabling easy visual navigation.

The same design approaches have been scaled to a specific urban context in the design of the New

Bispebjerg Hospital (2015). CF Møller worked with Australian architecture and urban planning practice TERROIR on the dramatic renovation of a heritage 1913 structure and a significant expansion of the facility. The close integration in Copenhagen's Northwest District and the adaption to the existing historical landscaped pavilion structure has resulted in a dense urban layout, which brings all functions extremely close to the green central terraced gardens that form the backbone of the hospital. These elements culminate in a multifunctional plaza featuring health-related amenities and providing activities for the surrounding city. Foregrounding nature and proximity, the project was granted the Architectural Review MIPIM Future Projects Award in 2016 for its ability to integrate modern and efficient care within small-scale and green surroundings.

A Completely New Approach

CF Møller's design for Denmark's largest nursing home, the Sølund Care Centre (designed from 2015), is a pioneering example of how city-integrated care centres can make it possible to give the elderly opportunities to live and interact with other generations. Designed to set new standards for

CF Møller Architects
with TERROIR and
CF Møller Landscape,
New Bispebjerg Hospital,
Copenhagen,
2015

A reinterpretation of the existing Bispebjerg Hospital's listed pavilion structure and landscaping from 1913, the 12 new human-scaled ward buildings, around a central terraced garden sequence over a base of treatment wings, are designed with an emphasis on light, air, closeness to nature and easy wayfinding.

left: The centre's architecture and integration with urban space seek to capture the feel of living in Nørrebro, while giving residents meaningful experiences in the form of closeness to urban life, light, views, and interaction with other people and nature.

below: Sølund is an ambitious pioneering prototype for the city-integrated nursing homes of the future, with an open and public ground floor centred on three generous courtyards, which provide sheltered meeting places for the multi-generational mix of residents.

CF Møller Architects with Tredje Natur,
Sølund Care Centre,
Copenhagen,
2015–

The Sølund Care Centre is a pioneering example of how city-integrated care centres can make it possible to give the elderly opportunities to live and interact with other generations.

welfare, wellbeing, security and functionality, senior citizens, young people and children not only live close together, but also benefit from each other's presence.

The nursing home is centrally located in Copenhagen's lively Nørrebro district. The project was won in competition by CF Møller with local urban planning firm Tredje Natur. Sølund's mix of housing types and residents is unique in a Danish context, combining 360 care homes, 150 youth dwellings (20 of them for young people with autism spectrum disorder), 20 senior dwellings, a children's daycare centre, micro-shops, cafes and workshops – a true 'House of Generations'.

CF Møller and Tredje Natur designed the urban spaces as meeting areas and social 'glue' based on the way the urban district already works. The approach is to simply bring together meaningful activities, while still allowing some physical distance between them. For example, the care homes and youth residences have access via intimate passages from the street side to provide a more peaceful main entrance for the care centre.

The main feature is the shared Generation's Square in the central courtyard. This is the meeting place for all residents and guests, and it is surrounded by a looped inner street which connects the various functions on the ground floor. This inner street addresses the community context with a hair salon, shops, cafe and other public programmes facing the urban side, with public workshops and rehabilitation facilities facing the calm courtyards, and a cafe and multifunctional venue located next to the daycare facility, facing a new lakefront pocket park.

By careful urban and landscape design, Sølund creates its own green cityscape. The facility invites children, young people, seniors and the elderly to be involved in shared activities, to inspire each other in the workshops and kitchens, or simply to meet across age divides in the numerous green spaces. These designed interactions create an environment where people in need of care are no longer excluded from urban life and distanced from their fellow humans.

The Big Picture

It is not a simple task to reconcile the qualities of the landscape-immersed and scenic Hospice Djursland with the new typologies of the highly specialised and city-scaled superhospitals. And the trend towards bigger and more centralised healthcare institutions is likely to continue, driven by necessary cost reductions and scarcity of resources, both human and material.

But as the quote from Hospice Djursland patient Lise early in this article shows, proximity to nature and a sense of place are so important to patients – and indeed to everyone – that it is imperative to find ways to combine these trends, as implied in the article's title: 'Lean, Green and Healthy'. The focus needs to be on the individual, his or her healing and access to daylight and green surroundings, while optimising the rest.

Using the evidence is an efficient tool to alter priorities in the healthcare sector and push the agenda. But just as the parallel trend to reintroduce nature in cities takes a highly multidisciplinary approach, this is a task that, in addition to the evidence-based, requires intuition, design experience and user involvement, as well as cultural knowledge and community involvement, to be successful in securing the bond between healthcare institutions, their occupants and broader society. ᗄ

CF Møller Architects
with CF Møller Landscape,
Hospice Djursland,
Rønde,
Denmark,
2007 and 2011

below: Cross section of the hospice, with patient rooms overlooking landscape, interior covered courtyard and staff areas towards front plaza.

opposite: Covered courtyard conservatories bring daylight deep into the building, and allow users to enjoy green surroundings all year round.

Notes
1. Dorit Simonsen, Rikke Krogager and Jens Oluf Bruun Pedersen, *Det som har betydning – en ZMET-analyse blandt patienter og pårørende på Hospice Djursland*, Boggalleriet (Rønde, Denmark), 2014, p 52 (author's translation).
2. On daylight and views, see: Bryan Lawson and Michael Phiri, *The Architectural Healthcare Environment and its Effect on Patient Health Outcomes*, NHS Estates project report, 2003; Andrew Symon, Jeanette Paul, Valerie Carr and Maggie Butchart, *Birth Environment Study: The Effects of the Interior Environment Design on Service Users and Staff in Maternity Facilities*, NHS Estates project report, 2003; and Stephen Verderber, 'Dimensions of Person-Window Transactions in the Hospital Environment, *Environment and Behavior*, 18(4), 1986, p 450.
3. On landscape and gardens, see: Clare Cooper Marcus and Marni Barnes, *Gardens in Healthcare Facilities: Uses, Therapeutic Benefits and Design Recommendations*, Center for Health Design (Martinez, CA), 1995; and Sandra Whitehouse et al, 'Evaluating a Children's Hospital Garden Environment: Utilisation and Customer Satisfaction', *Journal of Environmental Psychology*, 21(3), 2001, p 301.

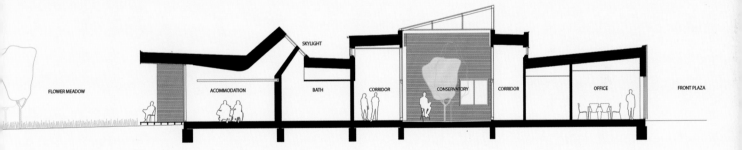

FLOWER MEADOW   ACOMMODATION   BATH   CORRIDOR   SKYLIGHT   CONSERVATORY   CORRIDOR   OFFICE   FRONT PLAZA

The focus needs to be on the individual, his or her healing and access to daylight and green surroundings, while optimising the rest.

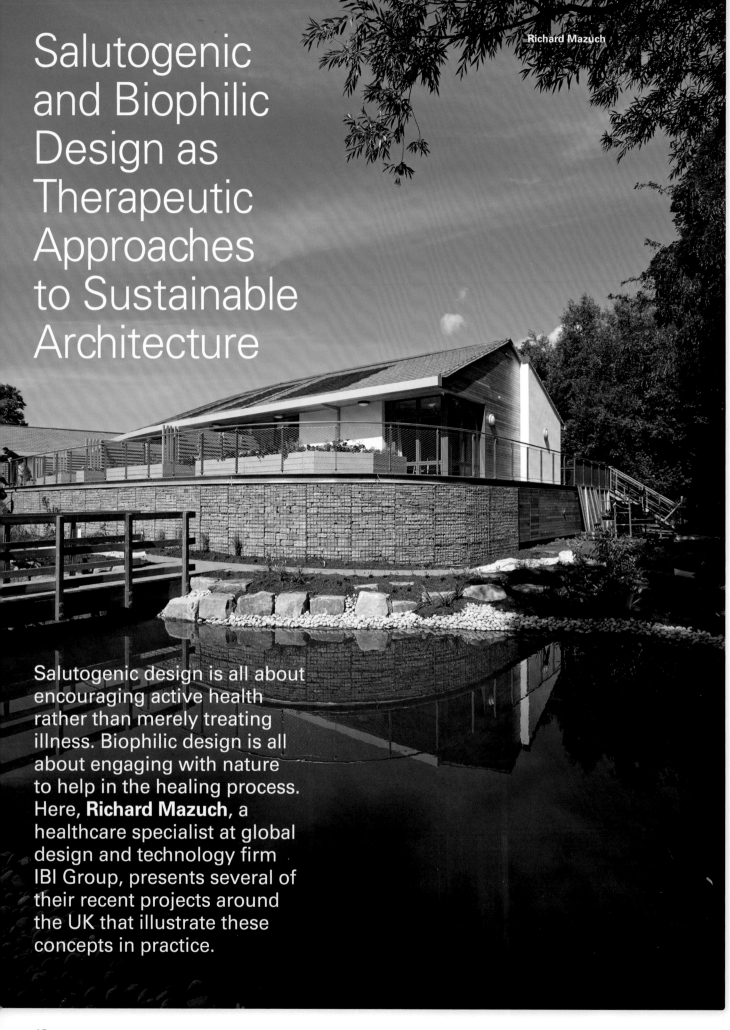

Salutogenic and Biophilic Design as Therapeutic Approaches to Sustainable Architecture

Richard Mazuch

Salutogenic design is all about encouraging active health rather than merely treating illness. Biophilic design is all about engaging with nature to help in the healing process. Here, **Richard Mazuch**, a healthcare specialist at global design and technology firm IBI Group, presents several of their recent projects around the UK that illustrate these concepts in practice.

We are presently entering the Third Era of Health where we are living longer than ever before. The First Era focused on communicable diseases while the Second Era, which began in the mid-20th century, concentrated on chronic illness, both of which continue today.

Chronic and lifestyle-related diseases are on the rise, and healthcare services are struggling to keep up with the consequent accelerating demand. Simultaneously we are finding new ways of taking control of our personal health and wellbeing. Increasingly the goal is to establish a long and fulfilled lifestyle addressing preventative as well as curative health management regimes.

Within this new Third Era of Health, the architectural profession has a very real opportunity to deliver optimal therapeutic environments that are seriously supportive of wellbeing, diagnostics, treatments and recovery in new settings such as the home and within the public realm.

Today, two key design movements are gaining traction in this arena. These are salutogenic and biophilic design. Salutogenic design originates from Aaron Antonovsky's theory of 'salutogenesis', developed in 1979.[1] The term translates into 'health origins'. Essentially Antonovsky, a medical sociologist, focuses on the promotion of active health and wellbeing rather than concentrating on the pathogenic approach that deals solely with resultant disease and injury. This essay explores these design movements in relation to current work by IBI Group, a global design firm with expertise in architecture, planning, engineering and technology. A specialist group within the practice is the TH!NK group, a research and development team dedicated to health design.

The Salutogenic Home of Tomorrow

Salutogenic design should be embedded in the blueprint of all spaces and aspects of our communities, establishing a healthy balance of mind, body and spirit that results in an overall feeling of 'wellness'. It is evident that national healthcare facilities are experiencing growing pressure with increasing patient attendances and the 'bed blocking' issues concerning elderly patients awaiting care packages. In response to this, there is much talk of the 'hospital at home' as well as the increasing need for people to actively monitor their personal health and that of their family at home. With an ever-increasing elderly population facing chronic health challenges and lessening filial support, our understanding of healthcare strategies has to be recalibrated. Indubitably focus must be towards delivering a service within the community: from assisted living, self-care, telecare and telemedicine within an evolved housing unit, to multiples constituting communities supported by social care services, nurses, doctors, physiotherapists, occupational health visitors, psychiatric nurses and local pharmacists.

IBI Group,
Kirkwood Hospice,
West Yorkshire,
England,
2013

opposite: All rooms enjoy daylight, fresh air, expansive views and connections with nature: a perfect example of combined 'living nature' and 'abiotic nature'.

A recent research project by IBI Group is the Salutogenic Home of Tomorrow (2015), which symbiotically responds and evolves to meet the ever-changing needs of an ageing population and its healthcare. This can be achieved in an innovative, elegant, supportive, dignified and exciting way, rather than appearing mentally and visually debilitating, degrading and stigmatising through the usual proliferation of awkward hinged metal grab rails, handrails, frames, slow-moving stairlifts and inappropriate, eclectic-looking furniture and fittings. Key ergonomic and anthropometric data will help design a supportive home with details, fabric of finishes, furniture and fittings, equipment and devices that will truly accommodate the ageing body – its predicted movements, weight, size, properties and cognitive abilities. A clear understanding of the ageing process, the maturation of the body systems, physiology and senses, together with a realistic comprehension of related medical issues, long-term health conditions/multimorbidity and salutogenic needs will inform the design of homes in future. Key design features of the Salutogenic Home of Tomorrow will include spaces for diagnosis, treatment and healing and general wellbeing.

New Technologies for Salutogenic Design

Technology and communication networks are examples of real-time clinical telehealth and telecare that can help alleviate the overburdened global healthcare system. Recently, IBI Group has undertaken a number of key telecare-related projects, including the designs for the Bristol City Control and Operations Centre in the UK (due for completion in 2017). This 24/7 telecare response centre will better integrate adult social services support with healthcare services for an initial 2,400 patients/clients and monitoring 13,000 connections across the UK. It will also provide mobile technology-enabled care services to provide support outside the home. Ultimately Bristol Careline will greatly alleviate the already overburdened hospital infrastructure. With high-definition video tele-healthcare systems, doctors and nurses will be able to examine patients and

Salutogenic design should be embedded in the blueprint of all spaces and aspects of our communities.

IBI Group,
Biophilic Design –
Nature Nurtures,
2015

We are hardwired to
the living world. The
phenomenon that is
Biophilic Design is a
rapidly growing method
of designing internal
and external spaces that
support the key healing
processes and optimum
wellness.

discuss their cases with them, miles away from surgeries or hospitals. Monitoring sensors such as tele-EEG devices and monitors can be used to capture and transmit physiological data. There are already early examples of real-time clinical telehealth such as tele-mental health, tele-audiology and tele-nursing.

Biophilic Design
Biophilic design is an innovative and rapidly growing method of designing the spaces within which we live, work, learn, play and heal. Edward Wilson, a Harvard biologist, first used the term in his book *Biophilia* in 1984, describing the genetic predisposition we have towards nature.[2]

Essentially the natural world, from which we originate, falls into two categories: 'living nature' that encompasses varieties of fauna and flora, and non-living 'abiotic nature' that includes water, sunlight, temperature, soil and the oxygen we breathe. A built project that embodies these concepts is the Kirkwood Hospice, built in 2013 by IBI Group, located in West Yorkshire, UK. Key design elements attributed to biophilic design are light, spatial permeability, sensory engagement, liminal spaces, organic shapes and forms, natural processes and patterns such as fractal geometry.[3] Usefully all these key elements can be supported by various levels of evidence-based research. This well-developed design approach ameliorates as it continues to be underpinned by ever-emerging research and more rigorous empirical data. IBI Group's Chalkhill Child and Adolescent Mental Health Unit in Haywards Heath, West Sussex (2008) is a good example of this, where the unique woodland location extends and permeates

through the spaces and across many interior finishes. In contrast, Ysbyty Alltwen Community Hospital (2008), also by IBI Group, nestles in the mountainous landscape of northwest Wales. Here the designers have harnessed the local metamorphic slate within the key architectural features, interior design, landscape and artwork.

The 'nature nurtures, macro to neuro' graphic (see p 46) lucidly illustrates the essential dialogue between humans and the natural world together with identifying the structures and building envelopes that interrupt this relationship. Natural elements such as sunlight have to navigate through liminal spaces, building skins, public to intimate spaces and finally through the sensory receptors. This exposure in turn affects our physiology, emotions, psychological disposition and ultimately our physical condition. It is essential to note that this may be further attenuated by illness and medication. Evidently, architecture has to deliver permeable design elements that allow this vital, beneficial and symbiotic dialogue to occur.

Edward Wilson stated that the most significant positive effects of biophilia could be seen in healthcare applications to ameliorate emotional and physical health. Physical environments have a fundamental and pivotal impact on successful patient treatment, recovery and ultimate outcomes.

Recent research supports measureable, positive outcomes of biophilic design on health.[4] Biophilic design can clearly improve wellbeing and wellness and can expedite healing within a world of increasing populations and urbanisation and increasingly hermetically sealed living spaces.

Researchers have consistently reported the stress-reducing and restorative benefits of viewing nature.[5] Clinical research has illustrated how viewing nature can rapidly reduce respiration rates, blood pressure and heart rate.[6] Early morning sunlight has been proven to reduce the length of hospital stay in bipolar depressed patients.[7] Another research project discovered that Bronshoscopy patients reported less pain when viewing ceiling-mounted nature scenes rather than blank ceilings.[8] Another research project reported that patients who watched nature scenes had substantially greater pain tolerance.[9]

Design for Wellness: A Five-Year Forward View for Healthy New Towns
There is an ever-increasing focus on 'wellbeing' and 'wellness' in the community and the overall public realm. Indeed, town planning and the provision of healthcare are united in being part of the remit of today's administration devolution. Though planners have helped reduce and mitigate the activities that impact on health, such as air pollution and noise, more recent focus has turned to the provision of infrastructure and services that have a positive impact on human health.

An outstanding example of this is the recent launch of the NHS England 'Healthy New Towns' initiative.[10] IBI Group is presently acting as key adviser for this programme and its 'Five Year Forward View'. The programme offers a golden opportunity to radically rethink how we live and takes an ambitious look at improving health through the built environment in ten demonstrator sites. These are located across the country from Devon to Darlington, covering more than 76,000 new homes with potential capacity for approximately 170,000 residents of varied demographics.

The intention will be to help redesign health and care services. The towns will be designed to address key issues such as obesity, dementia, mental health and ageing in place as well as focusing on physical activity, healthy nutrition and positive wellbeing. IBI Group is actively sharing its Salutogenic Home healthcare data with the towns to develop a residential prototype, which

IBI Group,
Chalkhill Child and Adolescent Mental Health Unit,
Princess Royal Hospital,
Haywards Heath,
West Sussex,
England,
2008

above: A de-stigmatising mental-health environment, using natural biomorphic forms and patterns within fabric and finishes, celebrating its connection with protected woodland.

IBI Group,
Salutogenic Home
of Tomorrow,
2015

below: The Salutogenic Home of Tomorrow – an IBITH!NK initiative – offers seamless support to multiple healthcare scenarios and patient types through its assistive design and technology.

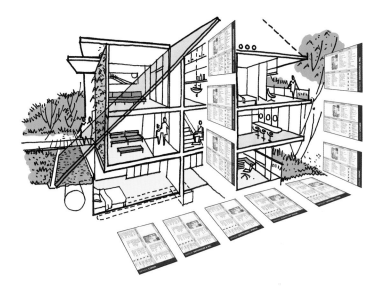

IBI Group,
Ysbyty Alltwen Community Hospital,
Gwynedd,
Wales,
2008

Sustainable solutions: the natural indigenous materials and organic architectural elements harnessed in the design of this healthcare environment relate seamlessly to their Welsh mountain setting.

There is an ever-increasing focus on 'wellbeing' and 'wellness' in the community and the overall public realm.

is currently under construction. This is usefully defined as assistive design and assistive technology. Ultimately it is the intention of NHS England to establish clear blueprint guidelines for future developments.

Sense-Sensitive Design

Inspired by the desire to create optimal, patient-centred healing environments, recent work by TH!NK highlights the significant and vital link between academic research and practice. TH!NK has developed unique design tools over the last 15 years harnessing the benefits of this evidence to good effect. Tools such as sense-sensitive design, design prescription, sensory plans and emotional mapping, all underpinned by evidence-based research, have informed the design of many projects addressing many varied patient groups.

Sense-sensitive design is a well-known and well-established IBI Group design tool.[11] Research into sensory healing environments has continued for over a decade in a drive to deliver true healing environments to all patient groups,

thereby reducing medical interventions.

An example of this is the Sir Robert Ogden Macmillan Cancer Centre in Harrogate, North Yorkshire (2013). This new oncology centre provides state-of-the-art consulting, chemotherapy treatment and support facilities for a very sensitive patient group. The building envelope takes the form of two 'pebbles' – a form adopted in order to reinforce the buildings' non-institutional character, maximise opportunities for views of external landscape and private courtyards and inform the patient journey through the various stages of treatment.

Cancer patients often experience environments very differently from other patients. Through treatment and medication, sensory receptors may become altered, hypersensitive or indeed muted. Patients may become sensitive to light and acquire a heightened sense of olfaction which can lead to nausea. Medication is known to be ototoxic, impacting on hearing ability and creating symptoms of dizziness and loss of balance.

Dysgeusia – a distortion of taste – is common, as is peripheral neuropathy impacting on the haptic sense of touch.

Design features and interventions within the project were investigated and harnessed to address these sensitivities, such as: sensory colour schemes; assistive support details; touch-sensitive fabrics/finishes; dimmable lighting; additional temperature controls; landscape specification; liminal spaces; long views; and odour neutralisers/emitters. Ultimately the project won a rating of 'Excellent' from BREEAM (the Building Research Establishment Environmental Assessment Method), certifying its sustainability credentials.

'Sense-sensitive design' is a rigorous, evidence-based design approach that identifies ways in which individual sensory receptors of varied patient groups experience built environments, thereby enabling the designer to deliver optimal healing healthcare settings. Studies clearly show that elements of the internal environment such as natural

IBI Group,
Nature Nurtures,
Macro to Neuro,
2016

This graphic highlights nature's dialogue through layers of building envelope, multiple spaces, anatomical, sensory and physiological body filters, ultimately having emotional, psychological and physical impact.

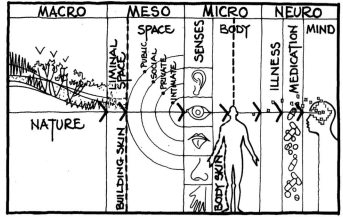

IBI Group,
Sir Robert Ogden Macmillan Cancer Centre,
Harrogate,
North Yorkshire,
England,
2013

The oncology centre delivers state-of-the-art cancer treatment for a sensitive patient group, while offering multiple and permeable views of landscape beyond and private courtyards.

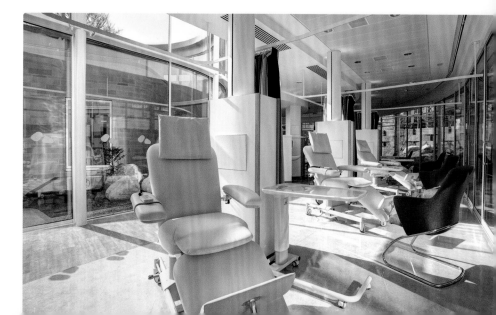

light, artificial light, views, art, smell, modulation of space and form, juxtaposition of furniture, manipulation of scale, proportion and rhythm, together with sound, texture, materials, ease and flow of movement through space and time, and indoor/outdoor plantscape, offer powerful healing and therapeutic benefits to varied patient groups. The radiology suite in the IBI Group-designed private clinic in Devonshire Place, London (2006) attempts to harness evidence-based research to positive effect despite the lack of contact with the external environment. TH!NK's aim is to build upon this research to create the most powerful healing environments for individual healthcare centres, departments, patient groups and indeed individual patients – from pre-term babies with jaundice to aggressive mental-health patients, from multi-trauma to diabetic patients, from cardiac to respiratory compromised cohorts and from palliative care to dementia patient groups.

Research into sense-sensitive healing environments has concentrated essentially on the five cardinal sensory receptors: sight (colour, natural light, art, views); hearing (pleasant or unpleasant sounds); touch (temperature, texture, humidity, pain); smell and taste (pleasant or unpleasant). However, recent findings have indicated that there are as many as 21 senses,[12] many of which are already being investigated in this design model.

IBI Group, London Clinic, Devonshire Place, London, 2006

This central London, windowless radiology suite offers choreographed procedures using a library of natural images, smells and soundscapes preselected by patients.

Meeting the Challenge

The 21st-century world faces great challenges in terms of delivering wellbeing and healthcare to an increasing and ever-changing patient demographic. There is conclusive evidence that proves how therapeutic environments help repair the body mentally, physically and emotionally. Remarkably, the very form, massing and orientation of healthcare developments can impact on patient outcomes. Armed with new technologies, innovative models of care, augmenting evidence-based research and new design tools such as salutogenic and biophilic design, architecture can positively step up to the plate. It can produce a new and powerful form of design that is not solely ocular-centric but is able to create and choreograph spaces that can definitely prolong life, heal and indeed help close wounds. ⌂

Notes
1. Aaron Antonovsky, *Health, Stress, and Coping*, Jossey-Bass (San Francisco), 1979.
2. Edward O Wilson, *Biophilia*, Harvard University Press (Cambridge, MA), 1984.
3. Nikos A Salingaros, *Biophillia & Healing Environments: Healthy Principles for Designing the Built World*, Terrapin Bright Green (New York), 2015.
4. Stephen R Kellert, Judith H Heerwagen and Martin L Mador (eds), *Biophilic Design: The Theory, Science, and Practice of Bringing Buildings to Life*, John Wiley & Sons (Hoboken, NJ), 2008.
5. For example: Russ J Parsons and Terry Hartig, 'Environmental Psychophysiology', in John T Cacioppo and Louis G Tassinary and Gary G Berntson (eds), *Handbook of Psychophysiology*, 2nd edn, Cambridge University Press (New York), 2000, pp 815–46; Roger S Ulrich, 'Effects of Gardens on Health Outcomes: Theory and Research', in Clare Cooper Marcus and Marni Barnes (eds), *Healing Gardens: Therapeutic Benefits and Design Recommendations*, John Wiley & Sons, New York, 1999, pp 27–86.
6. Roger S Ulrich et al, 'Stress Recovery During Exposure to Natural and Urban Environments', *Journal of Environmental Psychology*, 11(3), 1991, pp 201–30.
7. Francesco Benedetti et al, 'Morning Sunlight Reduces Length of Hospitalization in Bipolar Depression', *Journal of Affective Dissorders* 62, 2001, pp 221–3.
8. Gregory B Diette et al, 'Distraction Therapy with Nature Sights and Sounds Reduces Pain during Flexible Bronchoscopy: A Complementary Approach to Routine Analgesia', *Chest*, 123(3), 2003, pp 941–8.
9. MM Tse et al, 'The Effect of Visual Stimuli on Pain Threshold and Tolerance', *Journal of Clinical Nursing*, 11(4), 2002, pp 462–9.
10. NHS England 'Healthy New Towns' initiative 2016. https://www.england.nhs.uk/ourwork/innovation/healthy-new-towns/.
11. Richard Mazuch, 'Sense-Sensitive Design for the Ageing', in Lorraine Farrelly (ed), ⌂ *Designing for the Third Age*, March/April (no 2), 2014, pp 108–11.
12. *New Scientist*, 29 January 2005: 'Why you have at least 21 senses'.

The 21st-century world faces great challenges in terms of delivering wellbeing and healthcare to an increasing and ever-changing patient demographic.

Environmentally Smart Design

SHoP Architects,
HDR and Arup,
East River Waterfront Esplanade,
New York,
2016

Alisdair McGregor,
Ann Marie Aguilar
and Victoria Lockhart

Designing for Social Wellbeing Across the City and in the Workplace

The redevelopment project took a neglected
section of riverfront land in lower Manhattan
and transformed it into a spectacular
waterfront esplanade, providing areas
for active mobility as well as recreational
facilities.

Sustainable need not mean more expensive. Health problems caused by sedentary lifestyles, pollution and injuries from road accidents come at great financial cost – not just for individuals, but also for employers and indeed national governments. Built environments designed to keep people active and away from harm are thus economically beneficial, too. **Alisdair McGregor, Ann Marie Aguilar and Victoria Lockhart** of Arup cite some of the company's recent schemes in New York and London that have successfully encouraged cycling, strolling and other healthy behaviours, while also avoiding contributing to climate change.

Recognising that the built environment is a major contributor to climate change, the design and construction industry has committed to reducing its ecological footprint. Many new projects strive for net zero energy or net zero carbon – performance goals that would have been considered radical just five years ago.

At the individual project level, however, it is often a struggle to convince clients to accept higher upfront costs today to avoid severe economic and human pain in the future. Government agencies and corporations typically prioritise short-term performance, making it difficult for leaders responsible for the financial success of projects to accept these terms even if they are sympathetic to the goal.

But what if we can make the case that environmentally smart design can also help these leaders improve economic outcomes? Many carbon-reduction strategies also have benefits for human wellness and productivity, which has profound financial implications for the bottom line.

On the governmental side, the bitter and protracted arguments over how to pay for healthcare seen in many countries are evidence of the strong link between public health and the economy. Reducing the need for expensive treatments by using the built environment as a tool for preventative medicine could make a significant difference in national expenditures.

For companies, approximately 90 per cent of operating costs go to staff salaries and benefits. Investing in healthier employees, therefore, is a sound financial strategy. New research is also showing that healthy, active employees benefit their organisations in unexpected ways. For example, Marily Oppezzo of Santa Clara University has demonstrated that walking boosts creative thinking.[1] In an era when companies rise and fall based on their ability to respond to a fast-changing world, employee creativity matters. Rethinking workplace design to encourage people to stroll could therefore affect both short- and long-term success.

Arup,
Hudson River Park,
New York,
2010

The linear park provides bicycle and esplanade pedestrian paths, including the Manhattan Waterfront Greenway, to open up the waterfront for recreational use.

Carbon, Cars and Chronic Disease

How do we approach designing for sustainability, social wellbeing and strong economics? At the city and neighbourhood scales, a common strategy for cutting carbon use is reducing car travel in favour of public transport, cycling and walking. Because much of North America was designed for cars, this presents an enormous challenge. But in recent years both small and large interventions in urban areas have shown that it is possible to make walking and cycling easier, safer and more pleasant.

These low-carbon strategies have both direct and indirect health benefits. For example, fewer cars mean fewer car accidents – a hugely important goal. According to Sweden's Vision Zero Initiative: 'Road traffic is the 9th biggest cause of death worldwide. By 2030, the rise in vehicle ownership and use will see road traffic become the 5th largest cause of death, claiming more victims globally than AIDS and tuberculosis.'[2] Among the many indirect benefits of shifts towards walking and cycling are cleaner air and reductions in chronic diseases associated with sedentary lifestyles.[3]

SHoP Architects,
HDR and Arup,
East River
Waterfront Esplanade,
New York,
2016

Urban Interventions

To make this a reality, it is necessary to start with the individual. The goal of any urban planning and design intervention must be to convince people to walk rather than drive, or to enjoy cycling to work. For this reason, many successful car-to-active mobility transformations include cultural and recreational facilities along walking and cycle routes. New York City's Hudson River Park is a good example. In a joint venture with Bovis Lend Lease, Arup here served as programme management and design coordination consultant to the Hudson River Park Trust. The largest open-space project built in Manhattan since the completion of Central Park, the 220-hectare (550-acre), 8-kilometre (5-mile) long historical waterfront regeneration includes eight new piers, 12 park buildings, a carousel, tennis courts, soccer fields and dog runs. Bicycle and esplanade pedestrian paths (including the Manhattan Waterfront Greenway) span its full length, opening up the waterfront for recreational use. The park has proven enormously popular since it opened in 2010, providing a safe, efficient path for cyclists and pedestrians to traverse much of the length of Manhattan.

On the other side of Manhattan, the East River Waterfront presented an untapped resource to expand access to the waterfront and increase open space. Working with SHoP Architects and HDR, Arup designed a waterfront esplanade equipped with public amenities and a continuous bike and pedestrian path. A number of innovative techniques were employed to maximise limited space and overcome some of the site's inherent challenges; for example capitalising on the shelter created by the elevated FDR Drive, a new dog run, bocce court, basketball courts, cycle path and other amenities could be protected from inclement weather. To build a continuous pedestrian path, piles were driven into the river to support a walkway that carries users out over the water, not just alongside it. The project was completed in phases between 2013 and 2016.

above: The revitalisation project is more than just providing walking/cycling routes; it offers recreational facilities such as dog parks and bocce courts, drawing in a more diverse group of people.

below: The East River Waterfront Esplanade provides an environment where walking or cycling become the preferred choice over sitting in a car in the Manhattan traffic.

Reconfiguring Suburbia

These principles also hold true in the suburbs. The city of Concord in California provides an instructive example. Like many North American communities developed in the postwar era, it was designed for automobiles, with four- and six-lane streets lined by low-slung buildings. Recognising the potential for a dense, vibrant, mixed-use corridor around its Bay Area Rapid Transit rail station, in 2015 the city asked Arup's transport planning team to turn the surrounding streets into a pedestrian- and cyclist-friendly district.

In addition to generating economic returns, Concord's Downtown Corridors Plan will bring environmental and human health benefits; locating shops and offices closer to people's homes incentivises them to walk or cycle rather than drive. Converting a car-dominated streetscape to a multimodal, people-activated street, however, cannot be achieved through a single big change, but rather requires a series of interventions. One of Arup's strategies in its concept plan for the Concord project involves improving street ambience by incorporating natural elements, in this case bioswales and rain gardens that also serve as green infrastructure interventions. In the centre of the downtown area at Todos Santos Plaza, cars are not eliminated in the plan, but improvements to the street design mean pedestrians, bicycles and cars can coexist.

Arup and Vallier Design Associates, Todos Santos Plaza conceptual plan, Concord, California, 2016

In this proposal, part of the Downtown Corridors Plan for the city of Concord, many small interventions change car-dominated streets to multimodal, active thoroughfares that regenerate local businesses.

Healthy Offices

Walking or cycling to work is of course great, but if we then sit at our desks all day, have we really made any improvements to our health? At the same time as businesses are seeking to reduce sick days and employee healthcare costs through wellness programmes, innovative technologies are transforming how individuals track their health and the building performance of their homes and offices, empowering them with the data to demand healthier environments. Duty of care here is thus falling to building owners, designers and operators.

After just two years of targeted education, health screening and lifestyle support, the Arup human resources team has achieved record high employee engagement in its healthcare programme along with a drop in absenteeism and significant reduction in long-term sickness. Evan Davidge, head of the reward strategy in Arup's UK, Middle East and Africa region, describes how health and wellbeing discourse is entering a new era:

It is no longer a one-size-fits-all approach looking to enforce healthy options and dictate lifestyles, but about being true to our humanitarian company ethos and assuming a more nurturing role. The key is enablement: providing the tools, resources, and culture for people to thrive.[4]

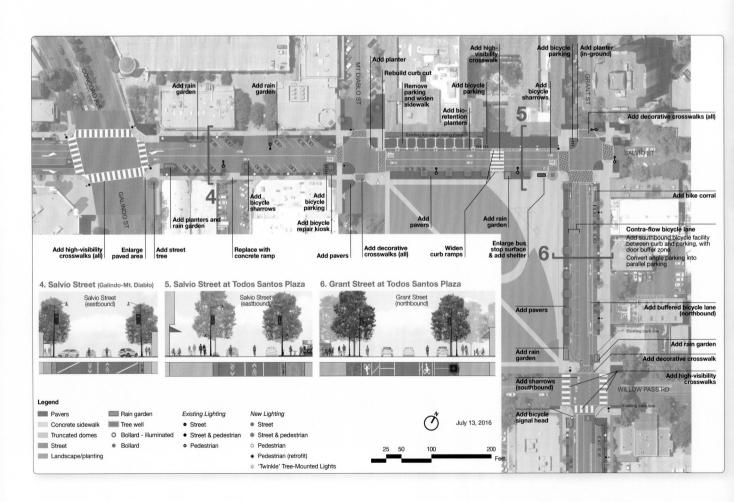

Arup Associates,
BSkyB Believe in
Better building,
Osterley,
West London,
2015

Ample daylighting and views to the outside, natural construction materials and multiple opportunities to work and collaborate away from their desks lead to a healthy working environment for building users/employees.

After just two years of targeted education, health screening and lifestyle support, the Arup human resources team has achieved record high employee engagement in its healthcare programme along with a drop in absenteeism and significant reduction in long-term sickness.

The challenge now is to extend the breadth and ambition of wellbeing initiatives beyond people management and into the totality of the workplace environment and employee experience. Our environment impacts not only our physical health, but also our mental state and emotions. The spaces we use therefore need to support the tasks at hand and facilitate healthier behaviours, ensuring that those that are best for us are also the easiest.

Active design delivers spaces promoting regular physical activity, whereas improved thermal, acoustic, ergonomic and olfactory comfort reduce musculoskeletal disorders, factors inhibiting focus, and chronic stress. This means that the traditional view of workplace efficiency where key functions are located as close as possible to employees' desks are no longer valid. Spaces need to be planned to encourage movement throughout the day. At the management level, following the research of Oppezzo, employees should be encouraged to go outside for coffee and lunch. In Arup's own offices, raised collaboration tables and individual desks have been introduced that allow people to either stand or sit to avoid the health issues associated with long periods of inactivity. As with urban reconfigurations, in redesigning the workplace small interventions can lead to large improvements.

In 2015, Arup completed the BSkyB Believe in Better building project in West London. A commercial building for Sky television, it was designed to be super-flexible to support the client's dynamic corporate culture, and focuses on creating specific, holistic, integrated conditions for optimising the health and wellbeing of those who use it. It is the first building in the UK to be designed in accordance with the principles of the emerging Well Building Standard,[5] key to which are good daylighting, air quality, and the use of natural materials. It is also a benchmark in environmental sustainability.

Arup specified materials that have low or no volatile organic compound (VOC) content to avoid off-gassing, and the extensive use of natural wood, internal and external greening provides human–nature interactions throughout the building. Designing a building where people could be active and creative required an integrated approach. Relating to the studies that have shown how offices can be designed to encourage people to stroll, affecting both the short- and long-term success of their employers, on entering the building an inviting, sweeping open staircase starting at ground level rises up through the triple-height atrium. At the first and second floors the stair width is increased to incorporate breakout spaces, not only providing circulation and visual communication across the floors and

Arup Associates, BSkyB Believe in Better building, Osterley, West London, 2015

opposite: The inviting stairway draws people to use the stairs instead of the elevators, improving health and reducing building energy consumption.

Arup Well Being Diagram, 2014

Diagram illustrating the different components of designing for health that must all be integrated to produce a holistic solution.

out to the plaza, but also creating the social and interactive focus of building.

The Way Forward

For much of the last century, urban planning and workplace design promoted a sedentary lifestyle. However, we now face the important challenge of reconfiguring the built environment to promote health. Arup's approaches to its sustainable designs for wellness and promoting activity encompass a variety of scales. The BSkyB project shows how flexible, daylit interiors are conducive to creative working. At the larger, urban scale, the new routes through the city, infrastructure works and related design strategies for Hudson River Park, and the mixed-use and green infrastructure approaches of the Concord Downtown Corridors Plan, demonstrate the importance of developing local responses to social and environmental contexts. In the future, Arup will continue to learn from a variety of interdisciplinary sources, including public health experts, to deliver projects that promote health and improve our wellbeing. ⚙

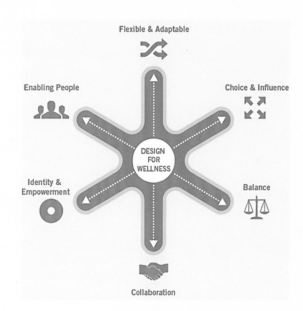

Notes
1. Marily Oppezzo and Daniel L Schwartz, 'Give Your Ideas Some Legs: The Positive Effect of Walking on Creative Thinking', *Journal of Experimental Psychology: Learning, Memory, and Cognition*, 40 (4), July 2014, pp 1142–52.
2. Vision Zero Initiative, 'A Deadly Threat: One Million Lives at Stake': www.visionzeroinitiative.com/one-million-lives-at-stake/.
3. See Arup, *Cities Alive: Towards a Walking World*, Arup (London), June 2016: http://publications.arup.com/publications/c/cities_alive_towards_a_walking_world, and Nick Watts et al, 'Health and Climate Change: Policy Responses to Protect Public Health', *The Lancet*, 22 June 2015, pp 1861–1914.
4. Personal communication with Evan Davidge, March 2015.
5. An evidence-based system for measuring, certifying and monitoring the performance of building features that impact health and wellbeing, administered by the International WELL Building Institute (IWBI).

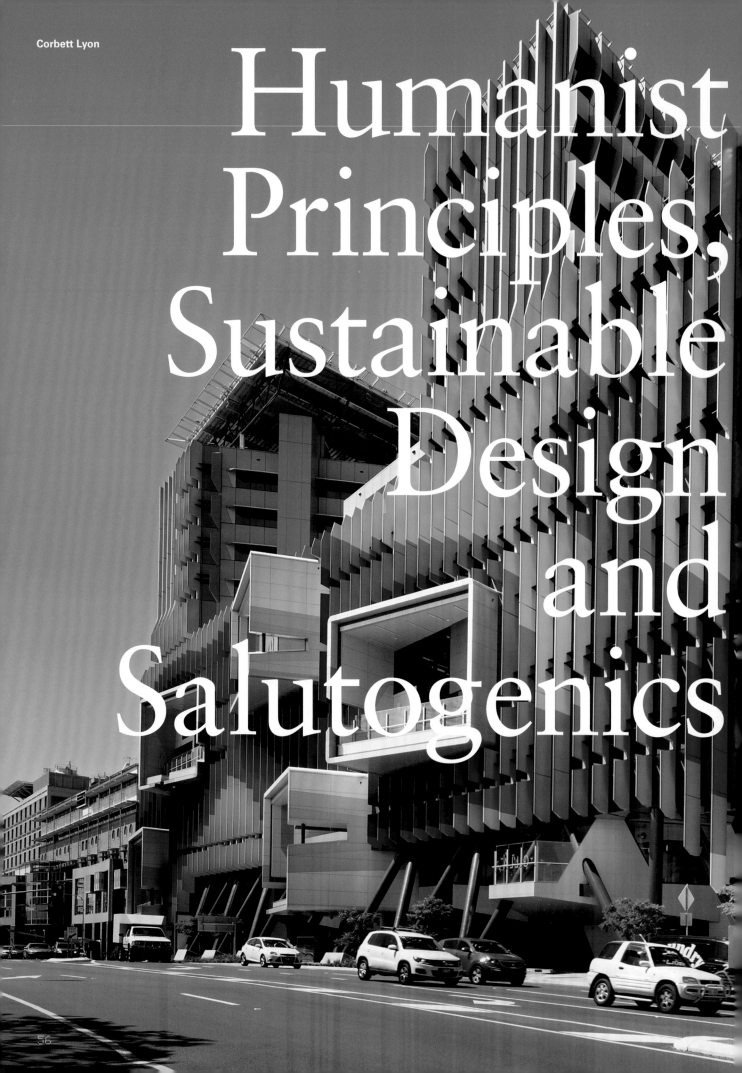

Corbett Lyon

Humanist Principles, Sustainable Design and Salutogenics

A New Form of Healthcare Architecture

Lyons and Conrad
Gargett,
Lady Cilento
Children's Hospital,
South Brisbane,
Queensland,
Australia,
2014

Australia's first healthcare
building designed using
principles of salutogenics,
focused on creating a
psychosocially supportive
environment for patients,
families and staff.

How can healthcare designers reliably cater for both functional needs and patient wellbeing? An evidence-based approach is the answer. **Corbett Lyon,** a founding director of Melbourne-based practice Lyons, explains how over the last two decades his firm has engaged with all levels of stakeholders – from managers, clinicians and administrators to patients and communities – to produce buildings that are at their service. After spending most of the twentieth century on the sidelines of this area of design, such research is allowing architects to reclaim a central role in a field that affects us all, from hospital facilities to care homes.

Healthcare architecture is undergoing a discernible transformation, as architects and designers re-embrace both humanist values and design as central elements in the planning of medical facilities. New hospitals are being designed around the social and psychosocial needs of patients and an understanding of their hospital experience. These facilities are increasingly incorporating natural light and ventilation, views to the outside, connections to green space, colour and spatial strategies to create healthcare environments that are both supportive and therapeutic.

Early Exemplars

Precedents for this approach can be found in European hospital designs from the early 20th century. Alvar Aalto's Paimio Sanatorium in Finland (1932) is an outstanding example. The building's plan articulated a series of private bedroom spaces that opened out on to extended exterior balconies collocated with communal spaces used by the patients' families as well as hospital staff. Painted in a palette of muted colours, the bedrooms incorporated bespoke fittings to support the hospital's therapeutic philosophy. In the early 1960s, this former tuberculosis sanatorium was converted into a general hospital, and in the process lost much of its original design intent.

Another example is Jan Duiker's Zonnestraal Sanatorium in Hilversum, the Netherlands (1926), which seamlessly interwove new therapeutic approaches with the emerging formal language, free-flowing spatial constructions and light-filled interiors of early Modernism.

Alvar Aalto,
Paimio Sanatorium,
Paimio,
Finland,
1932

Exterior balconies, views to nature, abundant natural light, and bedrooms painted in muted colours provided a supportive and therapeutic environment for patients in this former tuberculosis sanatorium.

The Medico-Centric Hospital

These early pioneering designs and the innovative healthcare philosophies they reflected were short-lived and quickly overshadowed by new approaches as the century progressed. Advances in medical technologies and building systems combined with a desire to treat greater numbers of patients and operate more efficiently, to produce designs that were medico-centric, where patient experience was subservient to the functional imperatives of the large-scale hospital institution. The role of the architect in designing and planning hospitals also changed, from one of central player and innovator to professional working in the margins, often in the service of functional health planners.

By the early 2000s, architects had begun to contest this increasingly accepted view of hospital planning and started to reclaim their central role in the design process. The re-emergence of design as a crucial element in hospital planning was supported by researchers in the fields of sociology, psychology and workplace ecology, who were connecting the patient experience with the planning of the healthcare environment. Evidence-based design emerged as a useful platform from which architects could confidently posit new ways to deliver health services and, importantly, demonstrate the value of architecture in a new, patient-centred approach.

Contesting the Type

The work of Melbourne-based architectural design and planning practice Lyons in the healthcare field over the last two decades has followed this trajectory – using design and design research as tools to interrogate and critique established norms. Its early projects involved typological speculations founded on the practice's research into the genealogy of the modern hospital as an architectural type.

At Sunshine Hospital in the Melbourne suburb of St Albans, the inpatient building designed by Lyons and opened in 2001 challenges the prevailing functionalist type of the hospital ward block. The building is conceived as having the attributes of a hotel – a place where one can come to rest and recover, not quite like home, but with the same supportive and restorative qualities. Generous bay windows in its facade, atypical of hospital designs of the time, create occupiable places on the periphery, where patients and families can sit and connect with the outside world.

The design also reinvests a sense of symbolism and civitas in the type, lost over preceding decades in the anonymity of the sprawling healthcare campus. Yellow and silver glazed bricks configured in a bold geometric pattern over the facade project a welcoming presence as a large urban art wall. The building form is curved and inflected to create an urban arrival space, a gesture echoed in the central spine and seen as a radical tactic at the time of its design, subverting the strict functionalist model of bedrooms arranged along a straight, central corridor.

The Lyons-designed Mornington Centre in Victoria (2007) explores a new model for the design of residential care facilities for the elderly. A series of workshops involving both architects and clients produced a plan in which the spaces are arranged to reflect the daily rhythms and activities of occupants. Aged-care 'wards' are replaced with domestic-scaled bedrooms with bay windows and openable windows, with spaces in each room for residents to place their personal effects. In form, the building resembles a large house, with an extended gable roof encompassing its residential programme. It is clad in patterned brickwork, imprinted with a digital design.

Lyons,
Sunshine Hospital
inpatient building,
Sunshine,
St Albans,
Melbourne,
2001

A brightly coloured, polychrome brick facade with projecting bay windows activates this multilevel inpatient building in the Melbourne suburb of Sunshine. The facade is conceived as a large-scale urban art wall, which can be read at speed from the nearby freeway.

right: The inflection of the building form and the curving of its central corridor were considered radical departures from the prevailing functionalist model of the hospital ward block.

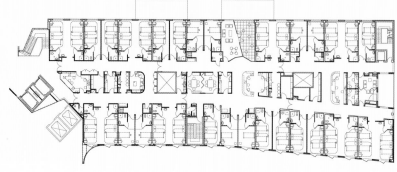

In form,
the building
resembles a
large house,
with an
extended
gable roof
encompassing
its residential
programme.

Lyons,
Mornington Centre,
Mornington,
Victoria,
Australia,
2007

In the planning of
the Mornington
Centre building,
healthcare design and
environmental concepts
worked together to
produce a supportive
interior and exterior
environment for older
people.

This building contests
conventional design for
residential care facilities for
the elderly through a new
typological hybrid – the
hospital and the large house.

A large gable roof
encompasses the building's
residential programme,
giving it a homelike scale
and form.

A New Era of Salutogenic Design

The Sunshine and Mornington projects were important precursors to Lyons's largest healthcare commission to date: the new Lady Cilento Children's Hospital in South Brisbane, Queensland, completed in 2014. A collaboration with Brisbane-based joint-venture architects Conrad Gargett, the hospital delivers quaternary-level services (the most advanced, complex and specialised forms of healthcare) to children and young adults in Australia's northeast.

The project draws on lessons learned from Lyons's earlier projects, and on a growing body of evidence-based design and research being undertaken in Australia and overseas. It is also Australia's first project to implement concepts of salutogenic design.

The theory of salutogenesis was pioneered by sociologist Aaron Antonovsky in his book *Health, Stress and Coping*, published in 1979.[1] Antonovsky postulated that a person's capacity to cope with stress was determined in large part by the quality of their environment – in particular, whether it provided a 'sense of coherence'. He defined this as having the attributes of comprehensibility, manageability and meaningfulness – principles that present an opportunity to radically rethink the premise for healthcare facility design. Rather than focusing on the causes of disease and designing hospitals that only treat sickness, salutogenics asks how healthcare settings can be designed to support a patient's health and wellbeing to maximise these qualities. Contemporary strategies to achieve this sense of coherence include spatial arrangements that deliver clear and intuitive wayfinding, the design and location of spaces that return a sense of manageability and control to patients, connections to nature, and giving purpose and meaning to each patient's hospital experience.

The design of the Lady Cilento Children's Hospital began with a process of active engagement and innovation with the clients, including clinicians, administrative staff, consumers and community representatives. Lyons used a series of interactive forums to challenge conventional hospital planning models and to open up the clients' thinking to the new salutogenic approach. Client representatives were encouraged to make diagrams of 'before' and 'after' scenarios as a way to describe the constraints of the city's existing paediatric facilities and, more importantly, to articulate a future vision for the new hospital. The resulting brief was for a welcoming, bright and supportive environment for young patients and their families, and a workplace that would foster collaboration between the hospital's multidisciplinary staff.

The building form and sectional arrangement that emerged from the workshops were not those of a conventional podium and tower, but of a medium-rise, sculpted form with a series of terraced landscaped roof gardens. The underlying concept and narrative, also developed collaboratively with the clients, is that of a 'living tree'. A series of double-height spaces (branches) radiate out from two vertical atriums (trunks) in the centre of the floor plan. Oriented towards major landmarks in the city, they provide views and a sense of direction for users as they move through the building's public areas, and also bring light and air into the hospital's central spaces.

Colour, natural materials and integrated art are used extensively in the new building to promote a sense of wellbeing, and to provide engaging distractions for young patients. Large-scale sculptures of coloured parrots occupy the central atrium, and images of butterflies, beetles and other insects are imprinted onto timber panels lining the public spaces. The colour strategy also contributes to intuitive wayfinding and placemaking, aiming to reduce anxiety and stress. The often impersonal and labyrinthine circulation spaces encountered in many modern hospitals are here replaced with a hierarchy of designed public areas – large and small, extended and contained, juxtaposed and flowing – all connected back to the building's treelike armature.

The colours used in the building are derived from clinical and scientific research into colour theory, and from the natural colours of the Queensland landscape. These include the muted shades and tones found in the landscape of the state's remote outback, and the more vibrant and exotic colours of its birds, rainforest butterflies and flora.

The hospital's facade serves as a bioclimatic skin, which responds to the city's subtropical climate by admitting light and air, but also shading the interior spaces from the summer sun. The colours used here are distilled from those of the local context – the vibrant purples and greens of the bougainvillea flowers that grow in profusion in the parkland arbour leading up to the hospital, mapped onto the vertical fins of the facade in a complex, contoured figuration. The fine texture of the fins also dissolves and softens the mass of the building; a colourful urban wall, it offers an engaging and positive contribution to the city's public realm.

A series of landscaped roof terraces and gardens are used by patients, families and staff for passive recreation, therapy programmes and quiet reflection. The green roofs also provide thermal insulation for the lower floors of the building, reducing the hospital's energy costs.

Lyons and
Conrad Gargett,
Lady Cilento
Children's Hospital,
South Brisbane,
Queensland,
Australia,
2014

The hospital's central atrium
features colourful three-
dimensional works
by Australian contemporary
artist Emily Floyd, which
provide orientation for
visitors and a distraction
for children.

This interweaving of humanist principles and architectural design appears to be a fruitful and optimistic path for designers.

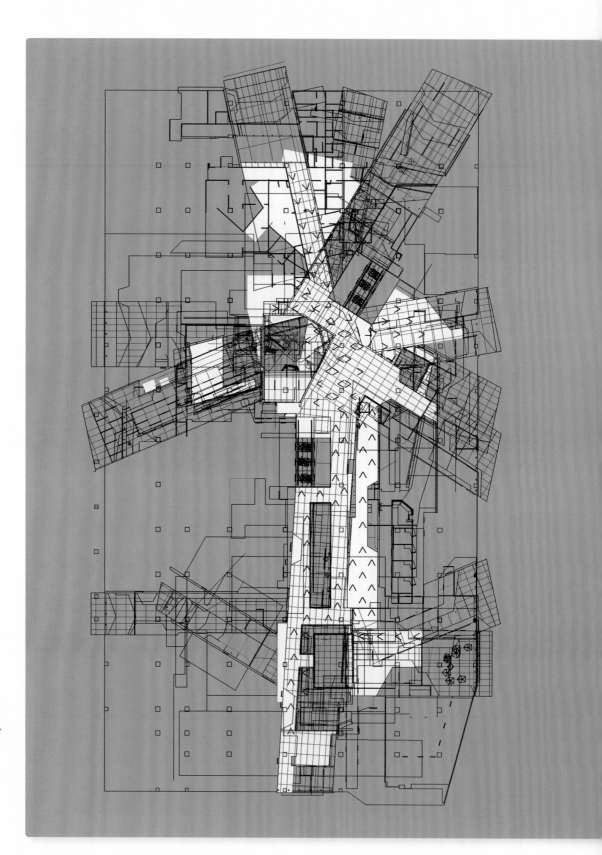

Lyons and Conrad
Gargett,
Lady Cilento
Children's Hospital,
South Brisbane,
Queensland,
Australia,
2014

Concept design drawing
showing radiating 'branch'
spaces that bring light
and air into the building's
interior.

The hospital's design also fosters future sustainability. The local climate allows for natural ventilation in many of the building's interior public spaces, with fresh air delivered through the ends of its 'branches' and through its vertical atriums. Natural airflow is regulated by automated louvres on the building exterior, activated in response to outside ambient conditions.

An Optimistic Path

Anecdotal post-occupancy feedback from Lady Cilento Children's Hospital users has confirmed that the salutogenic design strategies employed have succeeded in improving the experiences of young patients and their families, and in supporting the activities and work of other building users. Lyons is currently undertaking a major research project, in conjunction with the University of Melbourne, to examine how these design approaches, and their benefits for patient wellbeing, can be translated into a verifiable form, so that they can provide useful tools for future healthcare design.

Lyons continues to extend these salutogenic principles in its healthcare designs, recently returning to Sunshine Hospital with a commission for a new multilevel hospital for women and children, which is due for completion in 2019. Colour, form and spatial strategies are again being used to create a building that will be at the service of its users. This interweaving of humanist principles and architectural design appears to be a fruitful and optimistic path for designers, bringing with it the possibility of a new and meaningful therapeutic architecture for future healthcare environments. ◬

Green roofs and terraced landscaped gardens on the building's upper levels are used by patients, families and staff for therapy, relaxation and reflection.

Notes
1. Aaron Antonovsky, *Health, Stress and Coping*, 1st edn, Jossey-Bass (London), 1979.

Charles Jencks

Maggie's Architecture

The Deep Affinities Between Architecture and Health

Norman Foster/Foster + Partners,
Maggie's Centre,
Christie Hospital,
Manchester,
2016

The two wings shelter the main functions
so they all look out on greenery, the ultimate
linear solution to the same Maggie's brief.

The event that sparked off the UK programme of Maggie's Centres for cancer care was one woman's diagnosis with terminal cancer. That woman was Maggie Keswick Jencks. With her husband, the American cultural theorist, landscape architect and architectural historian **Charles Jencks**, she set about co-founding the pioneering project that has seen an array of high-profile international architects design acclaimed buildings where patients can face their diagnoses and undergo treatment in the most comforting and uplifting of environments. Here, Charles Jencks gives his account of the story so far and explains what it is that makes these centres so special.

In the West, architecture and medicine have enjoyed an intimate relationship since their beginnings. Imhotep, often called 'the first architect and first physician', combined professions in working for the Pharaoh Zoser around the year 2600 BC, and one can see why they are so closely connected.[1] Architects and doctors both are committed to creating a better future; they project plans and cures onto the horizon and seek to persuade people of their positive outcomes.

The close connection can be followed throughout the Mediterranean world in the Asclepions – health centres – some thirty of which were built by the Ancient Greeks, notably those in Epidaurus and next to the Acropolis in Athens. Their architecture was not just utilitarian but among the greatest of its time, and the open theatre at Epidaurus remains in use today, proving the point. This practice of expressive high architecture connected to healing continued from Rome to the Renaissance, but it was a tradition that largely disappeared in the 19th century under the impact of the mega-hospital. Maggie's, with twenty built over the last twenty years, seeks to recover this lost tradition – or at least I hope it does.

This is not to say today's factory-hospital is not productive. It is the solution to mass culture and technical necessity, the workforce and advanced machines dedicated to mass health. But Maggie's is part of a world movement (like the hospice trend) that seeks to combine the giant hospital with other building types and a more holistic approach. The forces for change are obvious. People are living much longer and will spend a lot of time in the hospital, visiting or being visited, and therefore demand a more varied environment. A typical Maggie's Centre is partly a spiritual retreat to confront some final questions, and partly an artistic background or studio for creation. It is partly a pub or place to learn relaxation and how to eat well. Or exercise together; and seek out information on cancer. Or carry on the twenty or so Secondary Therapies we offer as a backup to Primary ones, such as chemotherapy.

At Maggie's, we provide a place to meet together around a kitchen table, a focus where patients can learn a great deal from each other, and form informal groups. 'Kitchenism' is a name we give to this informality, and the kitchen area is the place you see on first arrival perhaps just after having been diagnosed with cancer. The big table is a place to have a cup of tea, providing a social situation into which you can insinuate yourself carefully, by degrees. Our group meeting areas, and flexible moving walls to service them, have opposite activities over the day and have to be so designed. Flexi-space and hybrid space characterise all our twenty centres, and if there is a common approach it is bespoke design, twenty different solutions to a basically similar brief.[2] In this sense the whole enterprise can be considered a postmodern experiment in a petri dish,

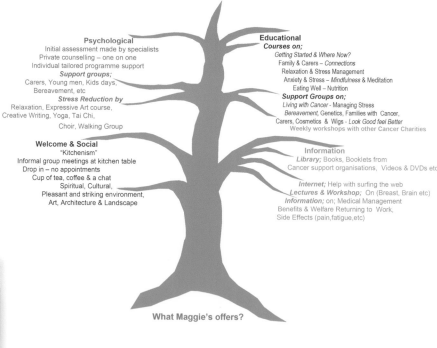

Psychological
Initial assessment made by specialists
Private counselling – one on one
Individual tailored programme support
Support groups;
Carers, Young men, Kids days,
Bereavement, etc
Stress Reduction by
Relaxation, Expressive Art course,
Creative Writing, Yoga, Tai Chi,
Choir, Walking Group

Educational
Courses on;
Getting Started & Where Now?
Family & Carers – *Connections*
Relaxation & Stress Management
Anxiety & Stress – *Mindfulness* & Meditation
Eating Well – Nutrition
Support Groups on;
Living with Cancer - Managing Stress
Bereavement, Genetics, Families with Cancer,
Carers, Cosmetics & Wigs - *Look Good feel Better*
Weekly workshops with other Cancer Charities

Welcome & Social
"Kitchenism"
Informal group meetings at kitchen table
Drop in – no appointments
Cup of tea, coffee & a chat
Spiritual, Cultural,
Pleasant and striking environment,
Art, Architecture & Landscape

Information
Library; Books, Booklets from
Cancer support organisations, Videos & DVDs etc
Internet; Help with surfing the web
Lectures & Workshop; On (Breast, Brain etc)
Information; on; Medical Management
Benefits & Welfare Returning to Work,
Side Effects (pain,fatigue,etc)

What Maggie's offers?

Maggie's Tree of activities and support

Maggie's Centres go beyond the usual remit of hospital buildings to give support on a variety of levels, offering a holistic approach to patient care.

Amphitheatre of Epidaurus, Greece, late 4th century BC

With its cosmic setting and superb acoustics, this amphitheatre continues today to be a site of comedies, tragedies and musical performances, just as it was when it was built, except without its hospital town next door.

with the individual styles varying across the spectrum, from disappearing background building to sculptural icon, and from green architecture sunken into an earth berm to a pinwheel galaxy.

For instance, at Maggie's Merseyside (2014), in Clatterbridge, Carmody Groarke have used six readymade Portakabins to compose an inexpensive haven costing only £217,000. By contrast, Norman Foster's design for the Maggie's Centre at Manchester's Christie Hospital (2016) is a linear greenhouse in a garden, the largest of our buildings, costing over £4 million. Different typologies also relate to different visual metaphors. For instance, Foster's building is seen as a 'wooden-trellis airplane, with protective wingspan verandas either side'.[3] Zaha Hadid's compact landform for Maggie's Fife (2006), in Kirkcaldy, is 'a black crystal' on the edge of a black parking lot. Rem Koolhaas's 'white donut', as Maggie's Glasgow (2011) has been described, is hidden in the last remaining woods of the Gartnavel mega-hospital. Kisho Kurokawa's 'spiral galaxy' (Maggie's Swansea, 2011) is very different in formal type from Neil Gillespie of Reich and Hall's 'Miesian box' at Airdrie (Maggie's Lanarkshire, 2014); and though set into the trees, Wilkinson Eyre's 'fractal treehouse' in Oxford (2014) is a different version of Piers Gough's 'Palladian treehouse' in Nottingham (2011).

Such metaphors differ as much as the typologies and style, and they show our hybrid building type to be what I call the small iconic building.[4] The iconic tradition, emergent since Frank Gehry created the 'Bilbao effect' in 1997 with his Guggenheim Museum in the Spanish Basque city, departs from the typical monument of the past which was based on customary signifiers that people knew well, such as the temple form and Christian cross. Today the iconic building, with its connotations relating to the cosmos and nature, is much more suggestive than denotative structures. And Maggie's architecture suggests why. When you are faced with cancer, a life-threatening disease based on rogue-life, you are likely to orient yourself to nature. 'Take your grief to the cosmos' is a Christian nostrum going back to prehistory; only nature is big enough to contain it. Such connotations and metaphors suggest why architects and physicians share their common professional beginnings: the orientation to a better future. 'The future is on the horizon', as the saying goes. Thus all our Maggie's Centres have both the big-sky view (at least through portholes, if not framed vistas) and the little contained inglenook, overlooking tiny gardens. The 'architecture of hope' is correspondingly one big orientation outwards; and twenty little foci on secondary therapies, inwards, our programme dealing with patients' specific cancer questions.

Maggie's Centres: different plans for the same brief

Layout is as varied as the style and metaphor, typical of postmodern mass-customisation. From left to right:

Maggie's Manchester (2016, by Foster + Partners); Maggie's Nottingham (2011, by Piers Gough);

Maggie's Lanarkshire (2014, by Reiach and Hall); Maggie's Aberdeen (2013, by Snøhetta); Maggie's Oxford (2014, by Wilkinson Eyre);

Maggie's Newcastle (2013, by Ted Cullinan); Maggie's Swansea (2011, by Kisho Kurokawa with Garbers & James);

Maggie's Cheltenham (2010, by Richard McCormac).

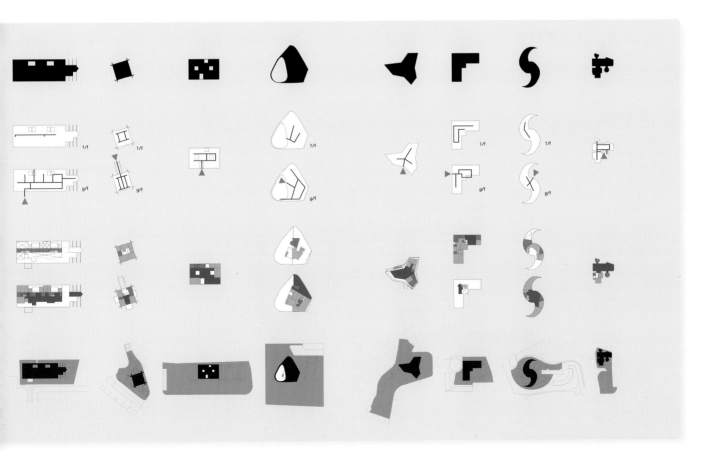

Haven and Risk

This little iconic building type can be minimalist and understated, or highly expressive. Either way a Maggie's Centre is a mixed metaphor that must both welcome in visitors and take creative risks. My late wife Maggie mentioned such varied attitudes as typical with cancer, as one fluctuates between preparing to die and fighting to live, oscillating between fear and tentative hope, and how hard this is.[5] Hence the architecture of hope must mirror these contrary and complex emotions, achieving opposite ends – standard practice for postmodernists since Robert Venturi's writings of the 1960s.

For instance, Ted Cullinan's design for the Maggie's Centre at the mega-hospital in Newcastle (2013) is both a stand-out sun diagram and a disappearing earth-berm design, a COR-TEN® steel structure recalling the tough local vernacular and a wood-beamed interior relating to the Arts and Crafts home. The L-shaped layout embraces the informal garden, with the low entry leading to an uplifting, double-height space that juts into the green heart. Theme and detailing are juxtaposed – ecology, solar power, flowers and garden versus black and rust steel. Unlike many architects, Cullinan understands plants and knows which ones he wants and what they need by way of soil and sun. Pools of enclosure have glimpsed views of the outside or a space beyond – the horizon metaphor again – and the kitchen table is not so exposed as in other centres, but placed adjacent to the garden behind a screening wall where group meetings can be more protected. It is worth mentioning that Geordie men collect every so often in one of the rooms

Ted Cullinan,
Maggie's Centre,
Freeman Hospital,
Newcastle,
2013

The drawing, with its 1960s ironic hippy sunflower, shows the idea of the centre covered with growth, surrounded by an earth-berm garden and a roof garden on top, with a south-facing solar collector.

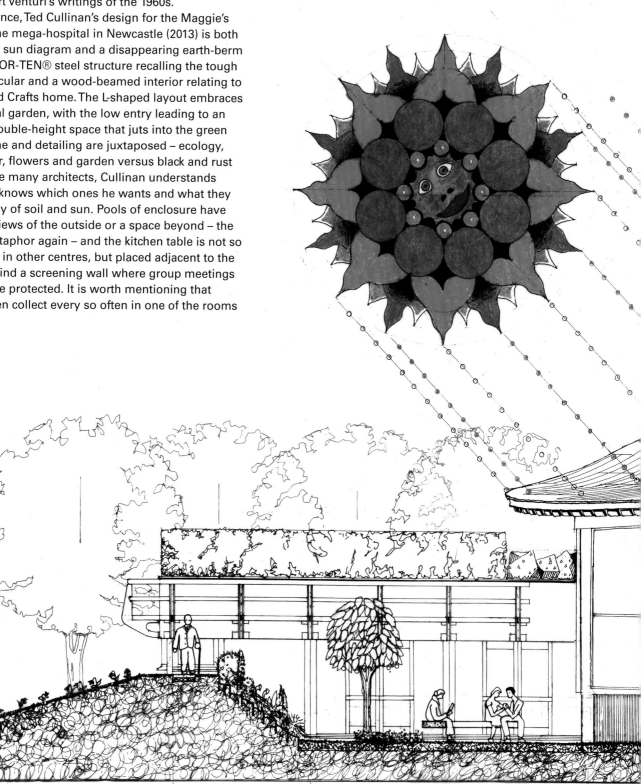

The double-height library opens onto the contained garden, while the staircase has inglenooks for reading alone.

(which doubles for art and exercise) to discuss their oesophageal cancer. They are a typical self-help group of patients around which the whole enterprise was founded back in 1994, when Maggie and I discovered that there were 500 such self-organising sets existing in Britain, often based around a particular cancer. Here these men trade informal knowledge, and call themselves by the ironic title 'The Osaphagoose', to mock and challenge their common affliction.

Cullinan understands plants and knows which ones he wants and what they need by way of soil and sun. Pools of enclosure have glimpsed views of the outside or a space beyond

Neil Gillespie/Reiach and Hall,
Maggie's Centre,
Monklands General Hospital,
Lanarkshire,
2014

Next to the car park and large hospital,
a walled garden becomes a building,
porous and protected, flat and stepping
down, symmetrical and asymmetrical –
understated contraries.

below: The brass lanterns
give welcome contrast.

opposite: Sitting areas are
furnished to give a homely
atmosphere, and the interior
is filled with natural light.

Several architects are developing the retreat as a model for cancer care, the defensive bastion which, nevertheless, relates to the immediate surroundings. Understated contradiction is a hallmark of Neil Gillespie's design, a Miesian courtyard house using a blond brick related to the hospital and Scottish vernacular housing just across the street. Wall architecture, perforated in parts and punctuated by midget courtyards with brass lanterns reflecting a golden glow, could not be simpler. But everywhere the grid is slightly varied, by a white concrete rill that becomes a fountain, modulated by artwork, or by planting or views out. It will not be noticed by the passing motorist; and, like much contemporary architecture – including Amanda Levete's Maggie's Centre under construction in Southampton – it seeks to disappear into the background, becoming Mies van der Rohe's 'almost nothing'.[6] Yet once within the walls, and on second glance, its minimalism makes the variation much more meaningful and striking.

Such opposition has been a guide for British architecture since Inigo Jones declared (and I paraphrase) 'ye exterior should be rational and sober, while ye interior can fly out licentiously'. Norman Foster's 'trellis-wood-airplane' (Maggie's Manchester) is, from the street, another understated wall building – a variegated hedge designed by Dan Pearson, and then the horizontal clapboard of a New England house. This inspiration from Martha's Vineyard is transposed to the wetter climate of Manchester, while the deep wings of the airplane have clerestory voids to allow in light but not rain. The fuselage is an ingenious mezzanine space running along the spine, giving extraordinary dynamism and dazzle to the interior. It provides a clear link between the office workers, above, and the therapies going on below. This close but separated connection has been achieved since the first Maggie's Centre opened in 1996, and it is one architectural aid to our success, furthering the idea that opposite characters make up an effective team, and that committed fund-raisers are as needed as carers.

In architectural terms, the crystal metaphor of the spine is reminiscent of E. Fay Jones's Thornycrown Chapel in Eureka Springs, Arkansas (1980), while it is here a giant crystal of a cockpit, not an altar, that culminates the route. This becomes a glass-enclosed dining space surrounded by hanging baskets and creepers for eating in the rain. It was also modelled on a conservatory Maggie had designed in Scotland, and it underscores the garden idea of the whole scheme, a haven of flowers and growth embraced by a hedge-wall of green.

Speculative Conclusion

Twenty years ago when we started Maggie's there were about thirty National Health Service mega-hospitals in the UK, while today that number has doubled. There is no way a charity can keep pace with the health explosion going on around the world, though Maggie's has become a model in some countries like Denmark,

Norman Foster/
Foster + Partners,
Maggie's Centre,
Christie Hospital,
Manchester,
2016

right: A view from the garden reveals the spine and its crystal-metaphor of skylights above the offices.

bottom: A sketch by Norman Foster offers various options of building materials and finishes to enhance the sense of connection with nature. Bare timber and glass predominate in this lightweight structure.

Architecture helps create the virtuous circle of the caring cycle but it is only an indirect aid, not a substitute for the ethos and commitment of those who work and play inside the building.

where Frank Gehry has designed one cancer care centre and the government has built six. The caring movement is a global trend, as I mentioned, and it begs a couple of questions.

First, what percentage of the factory-hospital could become given over to the cultural aspects of healing, those things that make disease bearable? At Epidaurus and similar traditional centres in Europe, the ratios of architecture to utilitarian building might have been four to one. Today the ratio has been reversed: if Britain's private finance initiative (PFI) is anything to go by, it is twenty to one the other way. How could this balance be reset for the next generation, those who are likely to live over ninety? In square footage the average Maggie's may represent one-fiftieth of the typical NHS hospital; but slowly the mega-hospital is moving along with world trends in a positive direction.

Second, for what other chronic diseases is a caring centre as crucial as it is for cancer; that is, for which of the big five conditions: heart disease, diabetes, strokes, dementia, obesity? When you have cancer you need a carer because there are so many physical, social, cultural and economic problems that plague you, and for many years. Furthermore, since cancer is a form of rogue-life that metastasises, one has to fight with proactive changes in lifestyle. These take long-term willpower and professional help. If Maggie's is a model for thinking about this question, it appears that dementia is the illness that really needs the backup of caring centres. Families have to struggle with it, patients make long arduous commitments to fight it, and the stressful dynamic between hope and fear is similar to cancer. Maybe someday they will get their new, caring building type?

As for architecture, at Maggie's we have found that it supports in the first instance the carers, and if you care for them with a good ambiance then they show up for work and look after the patients well. Positive feedback.[7] Architecture helps create the virtuous circle of the caring cycle but it is only an indirect aid, not a substitute for the ethos and commitment of those who work and play inside the building.

Postscript: Sustainability of Engagement

How does Maggie's relate to the sustainability paradigm? We have built green buildings recently – notably those of Koolhaas, Cullinan, Foster and soon Amanda Levete – yet maybe the s-word works for us in a different way. First, a word on anxiety-formation.

'Sustainability' emerged as a term over seventy years, when the H-bomb spectre of the 1950s gave way to the population bomb of the 1960s, and subsequent ecological disasters predicted by the Club of Rome in the 1970s. The discovery in the 1980s that the five mass extinctions were real – the last probably triggered by a wayward asteroid (which wiped out the dinosaurs) – was followed, in the 1990s, by the re-prediction of runaway global warming. Recently this possibility was held to be caused by yours truly (us, in spite of deniers). Yet many ecologists since the 1960s have often suffered burnout, because of protesting to little pragmatic effect.[8] In any case, sustainability is usually code for sustaining *homo sapiens*. This, in spite of well-known truths: that 99.9 per cent of all species are extinct, that the sun will become a red giant in 4.5 billion years, and that life on any planet is not ultimately sustainable.

Let all that pass; the fiction is well worth sustaining. In our case, according to a Maggie's Centre Head, Lesley Howells, what we sustain is the patient's continuous engagement.[9] That is, our programme attracts a diversity of people beset by cancer and, by working with them in self-help modes that I have mentioned, manages to keep them engaged so they come back, and take part in further activities. It is their commitment to variable and continuing self-help that is sustaining. Opposed to other programmes that may lose that interaction, our patients we hope will benefit the most because they are in it for the long term, sustained by self-chosen motives. ᴆ

Notes

1. Imhotep, ancient Egyptian meaning 'the one who comes in peace, is with peace', was an Egyptian polymath who served under the Third Dynasty king Zoser. Whether he was the first architect and physician depends on definitions, but a good case can be made, and was, by my teacher at Harvard, Sigfried Giedion, in *The Eternal Present: The Beginnings of Art and Architecture*, Pantheon Books (Washington DC), 1957, pp 269 ff; technically Imhotep is the first great stone architect, since many mud buildings came well before him.

2. The average Centre is 280 square metres (3,000 square feet). See 'Maggie's: The Architectural Brief', *The Architecture of Hope*, Frances Lincoln (London), 2010, pp 219–22.

3. This and all other unreferenced metaphors used to describe buildings here are my own, referring to their stereotypes and well-known associations.

4. See Charles Jencks, 'The Architecture of Hope', in *The Architecture of Hope*, new edition, Frances Lincoln (London), 2015, pp 25–6; and *The Iconic Building: The Power of Enigma*, Frances Lincoln (London), 2005 for an extensive argument about the origin of the enigmatic signifier and the new tradition of the icon.

5. She was given a death sentence of two months, prepared to die, then changed her mind – and mentions the fear of failure, a double death as it were. See Maggie Keswick, *A View from the Front Line*, ed Marcia Blakenham, published by the author (London), 1995, and later editions, p 11.

6. Echoing his more famous aphorism 'less is more', 'almost nothing' expressed the ultimate achievement in Mies's architectural quest.

7. For a discussion of Maggie's, a critique of architectural determinism and the indirect way architecture works on society, see my booklet *Can Architecture Affect Your Health?*, The Mondrian Lecture, published by the Sikkens Foundation, Idea Books, Amsterdam, 2012.

8. See my discussion of this warming runaway as the probable outcome, with graphs and examples, and the problem of burnout, in the section 'Critical Theory Carves Up Doomsday Fatigue', in Charles Jencks, *Critical Modernism: Where is Post-Modernism Going?*, John Wiley & Sons (New York), 2007, chapter 6. The two hottest years then were 1998 and 2005, now predictably transcended after a cool spell. With no global institution nor willpower, only false promises marked Rio, Kyoto and Paris. The Green Movement has to face burnout fatigue with every passing year.

9. Phone calls to Lesley Howells, Centre Head, Maggie's Dundee, May–July 2016. Her thesis has yet to be proven, but I'd bet that it is why we make a sustainable difference.

Sylvia Leydecker

100% interior (Sylvia Leydecker),
Rems-Murr Hospital,
Winnenden,
Germany,
2014

The subtly structured texture of the walls
of the patient rooms evokes grass moving
in the wind.

Emotional Wellbeing Naturally

Healthy Patient Rooms in Hospitals

100% interior (Sylvia Leydecker),
Rems-Murr Hospital,
Winnenden,
Germany,
2014

Sylvia Leydecker

Interior design can both support healthcare staff's working practices and help patients to relax and recover. A holistic approach is crucial: structural, visual, haptic and acoustic aspects each have their part to play. Cologne-based interior architect **Sylvia Leydecker** is a specialist in this field. Here, she describes two recent projects by her practice, 100% interior, where a sense of closeness to nature (inside and out) combines with cutting-edge technology and environmental awareness to ensure a positive environment for patients and their families, as well as for those attending to them.

Healing environments and the impact of healthily designed interiors are hot topics in the hospital world. This article will discuss the interior design of hospital rooms and the parameters which influence health and wellbeing generally, as illustrated by two recent projects in Germany designed by the Cologne practice 100% interior: a maternity unit in Essen and private patient rooms at Rems-Murr Hospital in Winnenden.

It is important to start from the patient's point of view. Sick and in need of help, he or she is likely to be feeling afraid and yearning for a caring environment. Apart from medical help, it is the sense of security, safety and trust that helps patients relax and feel better. Creating a room that really works, is sustainable and functional and offers an atmosphere of wellbeing for patients, involves much more than just a quick selection of colours, materials and furniture. It has to meet both emotional and practical needs, being easy to maintain and able to adapt to the future.

Given the global problem of healthcare-associated infections (HCAI), hygiene is crucial in order to ensure patient safety. High standards of hygiene seem to stand in contrast to an atmosphere of emotional wellbeing; but interior architecture in hospitals can kill people if hygiene is not taken seriously. The challenge is to satisfy both hygiene and emotional requirements. There is no need to view hygiene and atmosphere as mutual enemies: ideally the two can be fused together in a healthy patient environment that generates an experience of safety and security, resulting in a swifter and more effective recovery.

Studies have proved that contact with the natural world influences healing in a positive way and helps patients feel better. Human-centred design which is connected to the idea of nature is what this is all about: looking into lush green gardens, towards clear blue skies

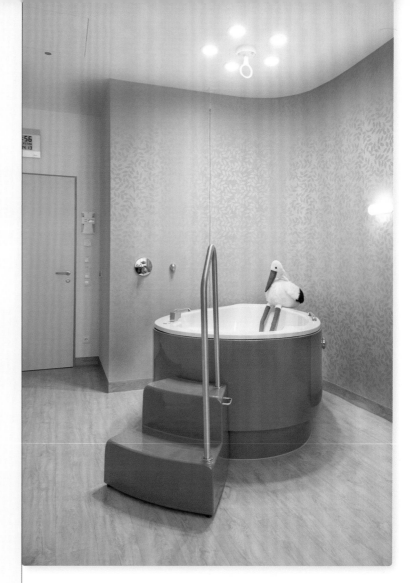

100% interior (Sylvia Leydecker),
Maternity Unit,
Elisabeth Hospital,
Essen,
Germany,
2013

above: Protectively curved walls give expectant mothers a sense of safety, helping them to relax.

below: The patient room is given an atmosphere of relaxing wellness through the use of natural lines and colours. The smooth pebbles symbolise patience.

or gently moving clouds; seeing a sunrise; listening to birds; and so on. Especially in times of sickness and fear, most of us need calm and safe places – healing environments, inspired by nature.

The design of healing environments that learn from and are inspired by nature is fundamentally based on creating positive emotions. Rooms need to be designed with a sense of naturally loving care for the patient.

The atmosphere of a room is usually created by the combination of materials and colours, light, structures and textures, forms and lines. Too often only one of these aspects is discussed; but in fact it is neither the colour of the wall, nor the comfort of the seating, nor even the wonderful view that makes patients feel good. It is the overall concept: the combination of distinct components that forms the particular space. It may appear easy to alter a room's atmosphere instantly by changing the colour of its walls with a quick paint job. But what about the other aspects: comfortable furniture; textures of walls and floors; view; light; air temperature; haptic and acoustic qualities; etc?

Light and colour installations that integrate movement and film can be pleasant to relax in front of, for instance in a waiting area. Artificial circadian light, mimicking natural daylight, in combination with soft colours and subtle movement, is even an option for intensive care units. Looking at cables and machines is frightening, so hiding them out of sight is the best solution. Noise is another factor that needs to be minimised, to help prevent patients from falling victim to delirium.

The absence of harmful components in paints, flooring, glues and other products used is important for indoor air quality. The environmental responsibility of hospitals should be expressed by an environmentally friendly production process – a must for a sustainable future.

Smart Materials

Times are changing and costs are shifting. Smart building materials can significantly reduce costs, such as those for energy, which is important for hospitals.[1] Deriving from nanotechnology – a key technology of the 21st century – they can reduce levels of consumption of energy and resources for a sustainable future. Even so, these materials remain little used in the healthcare sector, because of a lack of know-how.

Smart materials can provide a variety of functions such as self-cleaning, easy-to-clean and photocatalytic surfaces. It is important to distinguish between these types. Self-cleaning or Lotus Effect® surfaces are superhydrophobic, meaning that water forms tiny droplets and simply flows away. Because of their microrough texture, Lotus Effect surfaces cannot withstand mechanical exposure such as scrubbing, whereas real lotus leaves provide a self-healing effect when damaged. Easy-to-clean surfaces are likewise

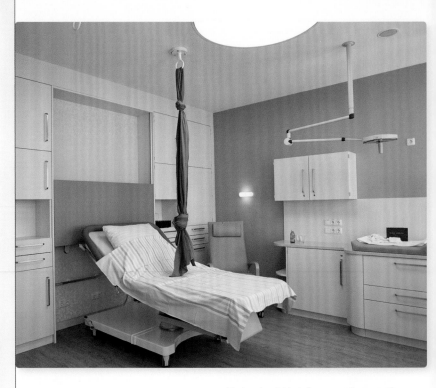

The interior of this delivery room fuses emotion and function. Soft curves, natural colour shades, hidden technical paraphernalia, a view to the sky: a relaxing atmosphere for emotional wellbeing. Furthermore it is a great place for staff to work in, as their working process was closely considered when designing the room.

Floor plan drawing of a delivery room, with limited space optimised for the working process. Round-edged built-in furniture underlines fluent movement through space.

Floor plan showing the layout and scale of the space. Space was limited and all rooms efficiently planned. Staff working processes are optimised, leading to an enjoyable feel-good interior for patients.

The calm atmosphere underlines patience as an essential prenatal virtue for both parents and obstetricians. This is symbolised by the use of smooth river pebbles, carrying Zen associations.

Hand drawing of the reception area which is far from feeling like a sterile hospital. Natural shades, organic forms and discreet lighting create an inviting atmosphere that relaxes patients and makes them feel more than welcome.

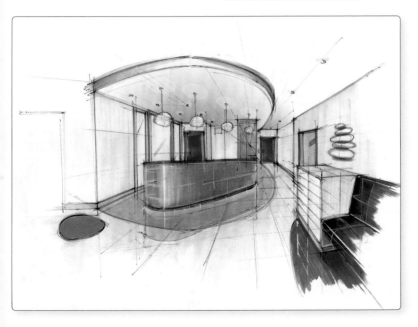

hydrophobic, but are smooth and usually include an anti-scratch surface. Often confused with Lotus Effect, easy-to-clean surfaces are therefore commonly used for sanitary objects. Photocatalytic surfaces, in contrast, are hydrophilic: a chemical reaction catalysed by sunlight removes dirt easily from a vertical surface when hit by water.

Integrating phase-change materials (PCMs) in walls or ceilings reduces the need for air conditioning to cool or heat interior spaces. Using light-emitting diodes (LEDs) or simply daylight lowers energy consumption levels for artificial light, and future organic light-emitting diodes (OLEDs) might lead to three-dimensional, bendable light surfaces that can take on different patterns, images, colours and light. Today's electrochromic window glazing can be switched from transparent to translucent: no need for curtains or energy flow. Antibacterial surfaces encourage high hygiene standards, bacteria prevention being crucial.

Interior design that results in sustainability and instant cost cutting is an option that should be fully exploited. A future-oriented approach to the construction of therapeutic environments can only lead to better design. Patient rooms and related spaces have the potential to be strong strategic marketing tools and USPs for the hospitals of tomorrow, conveying the soul and medical quality of the hospital.

Maternity Unit, Elisabeth Hospital, Essen, Germany

The maternity unit of Essen's Elisabeth Hospital (2013), designed by 100% interior for the healthcare service business Contilia Group, offers mothers-to-be an atmosphere of wellbeing and homeliness rather than of alienating sterility. It needed to provide high-quality medical care while incorporating a feel-good environment inspired by nature. The design process for the unit maintained a strict focus on the requirements of medical procedures, while never forgetting the basic aesthetic inspiration of wellness.

A natural approach was adopted, analysing scenery such as river valleys and asking which forms, patterns and colours appear there, and what their impact is. Wellness and the idea of a river meant total relaxation: no stress, but instead a calm, quiet, soothing emotional world for not only expectant mothers but also fathers, other family members and – last but not least – hospital staff. There is a close relationship and reciprocal effect between all individuals involved, and staff work more efficiently when not faced with frightened people. Most importantly, Contilia's maternity unit sets out to provide the highest medical standards, and so the optimum working methods are supported by an ambitious interior.

The calm atmosphere underlines patience as an essential prenatal virtue for both parents and obstetricians. This is symbolised by the use of smooth river pebbles, carrying Zen associations, as a key design feature that is found in various elements, such as the reception area and decorative lights. Inlaid pebbles as integrated wayfinding devices guide visitors intuitively towards the welcoming reception desk. The colour concept of soft, natural hues of brown, cream and sand dominates, while accents like soft green and bright orange freshen things up. Blue, representing water, together with orange, derives from Contilia's corporate branding.

Furniture was designed from start to finish by 100% interior, beginning with the optimum position of what, where and why and ending up with construction details such as fitting. For instance, cables were hidden from sight behind moveable covers: it was out of the question to hinder the maintenance of equipment simply in order to provide high-quality fittings.

Developing the tight layout was a challenge, as space was limited. The corridors and reception have no access to daylight, while all delivery rooms benefit from a bed with views of the surrounding scenery and sky, as well as a bathtub, comfortable seating for accompanying people, and adequate space to take care of the newborn baby. Hard edges are constantly avoided; instead, organic curves underline natural form finding. For instance the bathtubs are set in

100% interior (Sylvia Leydecker),
Rems-Murr Hospital,
Winnenden,
Germany,
2014

The generously proportioned patients' lounge area is dominated by organic lines that mimic the language of nature with softly rounded shapes.

A natural and clear colour concept in neutral shades enhances wellbeing, with fresh sunny accents in yellow and orange for mothers-to-be.

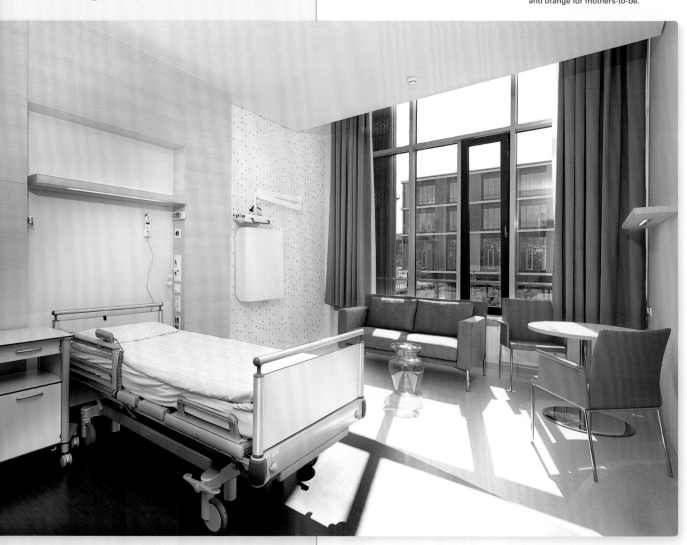

curved walls for protection: rounded corners have been shown to help people move around more easily, even in the rush of an emergency. A leafy wallpaper pattern decorates the walls around the bathtubs and also the entrance area, while corresponding accentuated lighting provides an atmosphere of wellness.

The interior design's therapeutic approach leads to a space which manipulates behaviour positively, inspiring mindsets of positive thought and emotional wellbeing.

The combination of bringing nature into the design while at the same time fully catering for the underlying medical process is fundamental to the maternity unit's success and high-ranking birth rate. Expectant mothers are more relaxed, less afraid, and furthermore attracted by a welcoming place, choosing to give birth here instead of somewhere else. Feeling safe and secure, with their loved ones and newborn baby, they find the postnatal recovery process in this healing environment is a happy one.

Rems-Murr Hospital, Winnenden, Germany

The private patient rooms at the newly built Rems-Murr Hospital (2014) were designed by Sylvia Leydecker, who was responsible for prototype rooms for Germany's private health insurance association, PKV. Most of the rooms are designed for general patients, while some are for expectant mothers. Some differentiation was required between these patient groups, but an overall concept regarding design components was successfully developed.

In tandem with uninterrupted views of the surrounding landscape, daylight and sky, a natural atmosphere is elegantly created through hints of grass and wood. Earthy brown hues and organic structured lines dominate the flooring, with curved wave forms adding to the natural feeling. A wave line separates the flooring of each room into a dark hospital-bed area and a light communication area with comfortable seating and table. Classy dark wood contrasts with the soft cream-coloured wallpaper, which is subtly textured with lines mimicking grass.

Note
1. On smart materials, see Sylvia Leydecker, *Nanomaterials in Architecture, Interior Architecture and Design*, Birkhauser Publishers (Basel; Boston, MA; and Berlin), 2008.

The lines are clear, organically structured and uncluttered. The discreet but striking colour and material concept proves relaxing and reassuring.

Youthful and fresh surroundings are provided for mothers-to-be, with patterned dotted wallpaper and accents of orange. Sunny orange acts against depression after giving birth. The changing table is placed in the centre of the room, in front of the cheerfully patterned wall, recognising the newborn baby as an attraction for visitors. A comfortable sofa provides space for visiting friends and family. Modern Italian design is present in the form of a piece of bright yellow transparent sculptural furniture that catches sunrays and creates sunny patterns on the floor. This sort of acrylic furniture is easy to clean, and it can function as a table or stool, depending on what is needed at the time.

There is a perfect view into the landscape from everywhere in these rooms, while mandatory curtains protect against bright sunlight and bring privacy. The best view is reserved for the generously proportioned patients' lounge, which is a great place to meet and enjoy a gorgeous landscape. Curved lines decorate the walls and dominate the seating. Nature is omnipresent and healing seems to be easy in these rooms, dedicated as they are to patients' emotional wellbeing.

Natural Design

Understanding interiors as therapeutic environments that offer economic productivity means far more than just nice, colourful patient rooms. Functionality; hygiene; working processes optimised by stress-reducing layouts; emotional wellbeing offered through natural colours, organic forms and patterns, and views into nature – all of these factors are key and demand a holistic approach to providing feel-good environments, without sacrificing practicality for the sake of attractiveness. Hospital brands require healing environments that have a demonstrable impact on people – patients and staff alike. This is what really works. Naturally. ◭

Transparent acrylic stool or table structures create sunray patterns all around and bring life into the space.

Can Architecture Heal?

**Michael Murphy and
Jeffrey Mansfield**

Buildings
as Instruments
of Health

MASS Design Group,
Butaro Doctors'
Share Housing,
Burera,
Northern Province,
Rwanda,
2015

Designed and built to retain
medical personnel and ensure
high quality of care at the
Butaro District Hospital, the
Butaro Doctors' Housing and
Share Housing foster a sense
of community among doctors,
patients and locals. The hospital
and both phases of housing
were constructed with the same
local labourers, techniques and
materials, a locally fabricated
– or 'LoFab' – approach that
reduces costs, invests in local
economic capacities, and builds
local stewardship that can
sustain the region for years.

In the work of MASS Design Group, form follows facts. Mortality rates in some of the world's most deprived areas are being exacerbated by poor architectural provision, which allows disease to run rife in healthcare settings and causes medical professionals to flee. Yet thoughtful design can improve physician retention rates, encourage people to seek medical assistance, and improve their health prospects when they do – all at relatively little cost. MASS members **Michael Murphy and Jeffrey Mansfield** here outline projects of theirs in Rwanda, Malawi and Haiti that have made an inestimable difference to the communities they serve.

In 1854, when Florence Nightingale arrived in Scutari (present-day Üsküdar), Turkey, at the front lines of the Crimean War, she witnessed the unique carnage that bad architecture could inflict. British military barracks and bell tents designed for deployable settlement were ill suited to treat the wounded and the afflicted. Leaking and overcrowded, wards were cramped, with limited airflow creating a chronic condition that caused more people to acquire and succumb to infectious diseases in hospitals than die on the battlefield.

Nightingale, a nurse by training and a remarkable statistician, recorded such conditions and dispatched her findings to London.[1] Her acquaintances at the British War Office ordered a Sanitary Commission in 1855 and sent Isambard Kingdom Brunel, a rising British mechanical and civil engineer, to address these issues. In contrast to the previous ill-adapted structures, in his Renkioi Hospital Brunel designed prefabricated pavilion wards that were not only deployable, but scalable and sanitary. With ventilating windows and optimal patient-to-nurse ratios, the pavilions were designed specifically to improve health outcomes. They were undeniably a success – the mortality rate dropped to less than one-tenth of the number at the British Army Hospital in Scutari before Nightingale's reforms – proving measurably that a building's design could actually help people heal.

Nightingale would later publish these and other findings in her seminal *Notes on Hospitals* from 1859. In it, she outlined the measurable impacts of Brunel's hospital and used them as the basis for a comprehensive guideline to designing the ideal ward. The guidelines recommended that wards, approximately 30 feet (9 metres) wide and no more than two storeys tall, be sited perpendicular to the prevailing wind direction to facilitate natural cross-ventilation, and contain what she deemed the ideal number of 32 beds spaced no less than 3 feet (1 metre) apart.[2] Buildings could no longer be considered mere shelters where activities like nursing

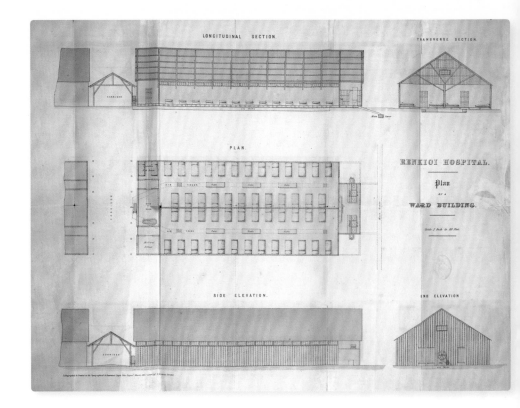

Isambard Kingdom Brunel, Renkioi Hospital, Renkioi, Turkey, 1855

Brunel's replicable, lightweight wards were designed to be prefabricated and assembled on-site in increments, allowing the hospital to be appropriately scaled for the number of patients it had to accommodate. Made of wood and covered in a thin layer of tin for insulation, the ward was well ventilated with openings running under the eaves, two long rows of narrow windows, and a rotary air pump at one end. Each ward was designed to be self-sufficient, containing its own lavatories, nurses' rooms, storage and operating theatre, and could be added onto either side of a central circulation axis.

or treatment occurred, and were instead thought of as participants in the care programme.

New theories about the effects of 'ill environments' on the human body caused architects to try to optimise space for health. Nightingale's principles, including narrow pavilions and operable windows, were used to disperse and manage dying organic matter and noxious miasmatic fumes rising from the earth. The 'Miasma Theory' held sway over medical professionals until around 1880, when more precise germ theory helped explain the transfer of illnesses from one patient to another.[3] Despite advances in epidemiology, Nightingale's model continued to prove so effective in dispersing airborne microbes by maintaining a sanitary environment and preventing disease transmission that it served as the standard in hospital design well into the modern era.

Form Follows Facts

For Modernists, form followed function. For Postmodernists, form followed fiction. It is fair to say that for Nightingale, form followed facts. She proved that it was possible to measure and analyse certain aspects of a building's performance to create a basis for architectural decisions that demonstrably improved health. With other reformers of her time, such as John Snow and Frederick Law Olmsted, she led what was called the 'sanitary revolution', a movement that promoted the design of built spaces as one of many strategies to improve public health.[4] It shaped our built environments in the latter part of the 19th century, and by the end of the century diseases like cholera and tuberculosis, which had eviscerated cities across the globe, were no longer a major concern.

Today, there is a new demand for a movement where form follows facts. Medical professionals, governments, clients, developers and communities want evidence and measurement of architecture's impact – especially as it applies to health – to prove it is worth the investment. Julio Frenk, the former head of the Harvard School of Public Health, has said that 'scientifically derived evidence is the most powerful instrument we have to design enlightened policy and produce a positive social transformation'.[5] Data can help us to design enlightened architecture, too.

Of course, facts only get us so far. Architecture's intangible qualities like beauty and idealism are also necessary for us to rethink and improve the world in which we live. Nightingale showed us that great architecture is functional *and* aspirational. Hospital architecture, in particular, provides the opportunity to make beautiful environments that improve lives measurably by investing in the dignity of the communities they serve.

Built over the last 10 years, the following projects by MASS Design Group pay tribute to Nightingale and strive to build architecture for the public good without abandoning the needs of individuals in the belief that architecture has the power to heal.

Butaro Doctors' Share Housing, Burera, Rwanda

Prior to the non-profit global healthcare organisation Partners In Health's arrival in 2007, Burera in rural Rwanda had very poor health indicators compared to other parts of the country, and was one of its most impoverished districts. MASS's first project, the Butaro District Hospital, built in 2011, was an important step in the effort to rebuild and sustain positive health outcomes.

Building on that momentum, MASS took on the challenge of improving the abysmally low physician-retention rates caused by inadequate living facilities. In two phases, the Butaro Doctors' Housing in 2012, and Butaro Doctors' Share Housing completed in 2015, not only improved retention rates but also attracted additional doctors, nurses and medical staff by expanding and diversifying local housing options.

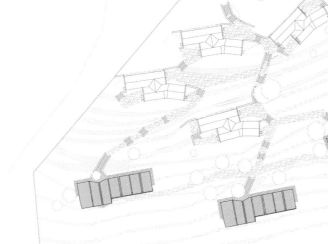

MASS Design Group, Butaro Doctors' Share Housing, Burera, Northern Province, Rwanda, 2015

The Butaro Doctors' Housing was completed in 2012, fulfilling a key role in retaining highly qualified medical personnel at the adjacent Butaro District Hospital. With the positive response of the medical staff, the second phase of housing, the Butaro Doctors' Share Housing, was completed further down the hill in 2015, with three additional units.

Site Plan

The three units that make up the Share Housing offer spacious, communal-style dwellings for a total of approximately 15 medical professionals, provide sufficient privacy and comfort, and foster a sense of community among the staff. The Doctors' Housing has contributed to the Ministry of Health's goal of developing the Butaro District Hospital as an exemplary teaching hospital and a model for holistic rural healthcare across East Africa. At the same time, through the irregularly slanted windows and the handcrafted stone facades made with local Virunga volcanic rock, the Share Housing continued to leverage the building process in Butaro to expand craft expertise and construction capacity, in turn engendering a sense of community ownership and stewardship. Butaro revealed that the healing power of a building also lies in its behavioural and systemic impacts on community and society.

MASS Design Group,
Maternity Waiting
Village,
Kasungu,
Malawi,
2015

Maternity Waiting Village, Kasungu, Malawi

In Malawi, expectant mothers face long walking distances through mountainous terrain in order to reach delivery facilities. This journey often proves insurmountable and prevents them from receiving care. The absence of professional medical care during a delivery is a key driver of maternal and neonatal mortality. In 2010, one in every 36 Malawian women continued to face the risk of dying during pregnancy or delivery.

Maternity waiting homes are places where pregnant women arrive a few weeks prior to delivery to await an attended birth. Housing high-risk and near-term pregnant mothers, they are a common intervention throughout rural districts in sub-Saharan Africa to encourage facility-based deliveries. However, data shows that this strategy ranges in effectiveness throughout Malawi and other similarly rural countries because facilities constantly lack space, basic comforts, ventilation and sanitation.

Completed in 2015, the new Maternity Waiting Village for the Kasungu District Hospital welcomes mothers to an environment that is sensitive to and acknowledges the risks and sacrifices involved in temporarily relocating to a hospital in the final stages of childbirth. The 'village' is aggregated

Lifted roofs at the Maternity Waiting Village assist cross-ventilation and manage stormwater runoff to prevent infection. Generous overhangs provide shading and shelter for the courtyards and walkways around which the village's activities take place.

from modular sleeping units that combine to form clusters of vernacular shelters and familial compounds that can expand around an extended column grid and adapt to site variations. Since Malawi's climate alternates between rainy and dry seasons, and because everyday life in the country largely takes place outdoors, the courtyards are arranged around protected outdoor areas where large roof overhangs also provide shade and shelter. Adapted to the lives of expectant mothers, they are centres of activity and learning.

Optimised for daylighting and natural ventilation, each sleeping unit thus prevents the spread of infectious diseases and provides privacy and comfort, while Trombe walls absorb solar rays during the day and radiate heat during the colder nights. Prioritising local labour and materials, including the fabrication of compressed stabilised earth blocks, masonry columns and locally sourced timber, minimises the maternity village's environmental footprint and supports its replicability as the demand for attended births in Malawi continues to increase. With these design strategies, the Maternity Waiting Village is poised to reduce maternal and infant mortality in the country and fundamentally alter the landscape of maternal health through a built infrastructure beautiful enough to attract the women who need it most.

Maternity Waiting Villages are designed to encourage high-risk mothers to seek care during the final stages of a pregnancy. A mix of enclosed, sheltered and open spaces provides ample opportunities for gathering around a shared experience, fostering a sense of community.

The Maternity Waiting Village is poised to reduce maternal and infant mortality in the country

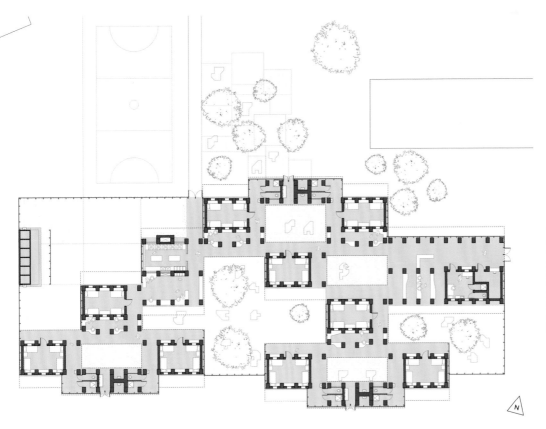

The modular, clustered scheme of the Maternity Waiting Village maximises access to small courtyards and patient privacy to encourage expectant mothers to walk about and remain on site, in order to prevent unattended births, one of the largest drivers of maternal and infant mortality in Malawi.

GHESKIO Cholera Treatment Centre, Port-Au-Prince, Haiti

In December 2011, almost a year after one of the most devastating earthquakes on record, a cholera outbreak in Port-au-Prince exposed the staggering lack of basic services, including electricity, running water, sewage and waste management in the temporary relief encampments. This foreboding gap in sanitation posed a significant public health risk that was threatening the entire country.

To mitigate and control the outbreak, MASS collaborated with Les Centres GHESKIO,[6] a Haitian health-services organisation specialising in infectious diseases, on a Cholera Treatment Centre in the city. Through strategic drainage, filtration, daylighting and low-energy fans that facilitate natural ventilation, the building is optimised to contain and manage an epidemic. Because the social stigma associated with cholera can discourage people from

MASS Design Group,
GHESKIO Cholera
Treatment Centre,
Port-au-Prince,
Haiti,
2015

The perforated facade offers ample daylighting and ventilation while also ensuring patient privacy and comfort in a sustainable environment designed for positive health outcomes as well as dignity.

Facilities such as the Cholera Treatment Centre will help Haiti attract and retain intellectual resources, local investment and human capital.

Design strategies including expansive ceilings, ample daylighting, interior vegetation and cross-ventilation create a patient environment that prioritises comfort and dignity.

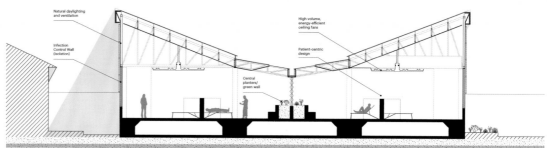

A - A'   Strategies for patient comfort and dignity

Designed to collect, store and recycle rainwater in planters and throughout the facility, the centre also recycles and treats wastewater to avoid recontamination of the water table, ensuring a sanitary and sustainable future for the facility and the city.

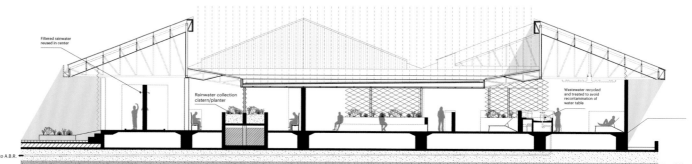

B - B'   Strategies for water recycling, reuse, and treatment

seeking treatment, it was important that the design provide privacy, comfort and dignity. A perforated metal screen modulated to maximise airflow and reduce heat within the facility offers a beautiful, well-ventilated atmosphere without compromising patient privacy. While patients receive proper care, an on-site wastewater treatment facility prevents recontamination of the water table and contains the spread of the disease.

Healthcare delivery in Haiti suffers from a persistent struggle to retain the doctors, nurses and other healthcare professionals it trains. Despite having five medical schools, and a continuing need for highly qualified medical professionals, most of the country's doctors flee. In a *New York Times* interview, the founder of GHESKIO, Dr Jean Pape, explained: 'Architecture and health are inseparable. A building that is ugly, with no fresh air, no dignity or common sense, is a place people will avoid, and this encourages epidemics.'[7] Designed for health and sustainability, facilities such as the Cholera Treatment Centre in Port-Au-Prince will help Haiti attract and retain intellectual resources, local investment and human capital.

Designing for Measurable Outcomes

Nightingale's data-driven observations and recommendations demonstrated a relationship between architecture and health. The recent MASS projects described here show that architecture can help improve retention of doctors and other medical staff, reduce maternal mortality, and mitigate waterborne disease transfer and death. Leveraging the design process to achieve measurable health outcomes, each reveals architecture's broader potential to promote sustainable physical, emotional, social, economic or environmental health. ⌂

Notes

1. Nightingale's statistics and findings are reflected in the *Report upon the State of the Hospitals of the British Army in the Crimea and Scutari*, George Edward Eyre and William Spottiswoode (London), 1855.
2. Florence Nightingale, *Notes on Hospitals*, 3rd edn, Longman, Green, Longman, Roberts, and Green (London), 1863, pp 13–16, 58–64.
3. Arthur Silverstein, *A History of Immunology*, Academic Press (Boston, MA), 1989, pp 40–41.
4. Thomas Fisher, 'Frederick Law Olmsted and the Campaign for Public Health', *Places Journal*, November 2010: https://placesjournal.org/article/frederick-law-olmsted-and-the-campaign-for-public-health/.
5. Dr Julio Frenk, quoted in Jonathan Shaw, 'Why "Big Data" is a Big Deal', *The Harvard Magazine*, March–April 2014: http://harvardmagazine.com/2014/03/why-big-data-is-a-big-deal#article-images.
6. GHESKIO is the French acronym for the Haitian Group for the Study of Kaposi's Sarcoma and Opportunistic Infections.
7. Dr Jean Pape, quoted in Michael Kimmelman, 'In Haiti, Battling Disease with Open-Air Clinics', *The New York Times*, 28 December 2014: www.nytimes.com/2014/12/29/arts/design/in-haiti-battling-disease-with-open-air-clinics.html?_r=0.

① WATER COLLECTION SYSTEM

Rainwater is collected along the center of the roof and is channeled along a runnel to the northwest edge, where it drains into a tank built into a planter within the building.

② CISTERN

The water collected from the roof into the storage tank at grade is pumped to a rooftop cistern on the building adjacent of the CTC for storage, filtering and reuse within the treatment center.

③ O.R.S. (Oral Rehydration Solution)

The filtered rainwater from the cistern is piped back into the CTC, where it is mixed with salts to act as a rapid rehydration tool for patients.

④ A.B.R.(Anaerobic Baffled Reactor)

Wastewater is piped from the CTC into a 4-chambered Anaerobic Baffled Reactor, where the waste is broken down into biomass sludge and fertigation water to be used on the site.

⑤ LEACHING FIELD

The treated wastewater is irrigated into a leaching field adjacent to the CTC, where it soaks into the groundwater, with further impurities removed by the plant life.

In the aftermath of the cholera outbreak that struck Port-au-Prince after the 2010 earthquake, the public health demands of containing the spread of a waterborne infectious disease drove the need to design the Cholera Treatment Center as a sustainable, self-contained system that collects, stores, filters and uses rainwater productively on site.

Sean Ahlquist, Leah Ketcheson
and Costanza Colombi

The Dynamic Interplay of Environment, Movement and Social Function

Multisensory

Sean Ahlquist, Costanza Colombi, Leah Ketcheson and
Oliver Popadich, Sensory Surface – StretchCOLOR prototype,
Taubman College of Architecture and Urban Planning,
University of Michigan, Ann Arbor, Michigan, 2016

The CNC-knitted textile is calibrated to enhance sensory perception across the
spectrum of tactile receptors, from skin, to muscles and joints. The visual projections
on the textile enhance the understanding of movement by grading colours based
upon amount of pressured applied.

Early difficulties with motor skills are a common indicator of autism. Overcoming these can improve both the health and the social opportunities of those affected. **Sean Ahlquist, Leah Ketcheson and Costanza Colombi** – respectively academic specialists in architecture, kinesiology and psychiatry – here describe their cross-departmental collaboration at the University of Michigan which aims to do just that, through specially designed interactive sensory environments.

Architecture

Architecture based upon materials research has long pursued the precise alignment of computational design processes, advanced manufacturing methodologies and technical performance. The research described here, a collaboration between the Taubman College of Architecture and Urban Planning, Department of Psychiatry and School of Kinesiology at the University of Michigan, expands this practice by exploring the experiential and sensorial nature of a series of prototypes developed as multisensory architectures for children with autism spectrum disorder (ASD).

Bringing together materials research and new kinaesthetic therapies, the spatial experience and modes of interaction of the prototypes are designed to address social, communicational and motor-based challenges. As part of an ongoing pilot study, the prototypes are being installed at various therapy centres to engage children with ASD and hence to understand their skill-building capacities.

The structures explore the significance of advancing spatial concepts and materials technologies towards forming malleable, adaptive architectures. In relation to sustainability, the concept of environmental specificity shifts from site to human experience. The architecture is asked to accommodate an individually variable sensorial experience, to provide a productive mode of therapy, and to explore the relationship of both to a child's behavioural patterns. Central to the proposition of the research is the design agency that emerges from the explicit production of materials differentiation. Conventional methods often produce differentiation through the modification, or post-processing, of homogenous materials. By contrast, when operating at the finest scales of organising matter into material, a more intimate and instrumental control over material expression emerges.[1]

Instrumentalising greater hierarchies of materials and scales of fabrication allows the concepts of a material-driven architecture to increasingly expand, capturing parameters of the immaterial, the multivalent and the extra-systemic. This is exemplified in the Sensory Surface and Sensory Playscape prototypes developed as part of the research at the University of Michigan. As environments formed by textile and fibre-based materials, elasticity is the operable material behaviour. The Surface prototype, a two-dimensional textile interface, targets the grading of motor control. The Playscape prototype, a three-dimensional textile environment, focuses on reinforcing communication and the successes of social play through variable multisensory experiences.

Behaviour and Environment

In the experience of space and time, perception is formed through the seamless integration of initially segregated data regarding internal and external, social and non-social stimuli. It is the interpretation of such stimuli, defining hierarchies and associations that forms the foundation of a coordinated and appropriate response to the complex multimodal (multisensory) data. A characteristic of autism is a lack of ability to filter, sort and integrate the ongoing pulses of such data.[2] For a person with autism, the experience of an environment is often defined by a singular magnified sensorial stimulus. The preference to a select stimulus significantly factors into the level of behavioural regulation and limits of social functioning within their environment.

Touch and reactivity to tactile stimuli are critical features in processing and forming responses to our environment and social interactions. Atypical tactile responsiveness is often a characteristic in children with autism.[3] Sensory seeking, for example, manifests as a craving for specific, often intense sensory inputs. Abnormal processing of sensory stimuli is seen to correlate with reduced social attention and impairments in social interaction and nonverbal communication.[4] A person's selective sensory function poses a challenge for them to achieve a positive sensory reinforcement for the complex and diverse stimuli associated with social interaction.

The point of intervention in affecting the relationship between environment and behaviour is pivotal in addressing aberrations in the socio-sensory link. Stress for a child with ASD may emanate from the mismatch between environment and the processing of its myriad stimuli. However, it is in the manipulation of environment where successful intervention can occur, instead of focusing on eliminating the atypical mechanisms of sensory processing.[5] Thus emerges the necessity for architectures to be subservient to the individualistic and temporal nature of sensory perception of space and experience.

As a part of an initial pilot study, Sean Ahlquist's daughter, a six-year-old with autism spectrum disorder (ASD), tests the Sensory Surface prototype. The StretchCOLOR bespoke software enables a tactile experience for colouring. Addressing limited control over grading of movement, changes in pressure on the CNC-knitted textile activate different colours to be projected onto the surface.

Sean Ahlquist,
Costanza Colombi,
Leah Ketcheson,
Oliver Popadich
and Disha Sharmin,
Sensory Playscape –
StretchSWARM prototype,
HandsOn Museum,
Ann Arbor,
Michigan,
2016

The textile hybrid structure and swarm-based interface, programmed in Unity, generate an environment that is highly tuneable in its physical, tactile, visual and auditory expression. The Sensory Playscape prototype, tested here during a sensory-friendly event for children with autism at the Ann Arbor HandsOn Museum, was developed collaboratively as part of the Tactile Interfaces and Environments project funded by an MCubed grant for interdisciplinary research from the University of Michigan.

Perception is formed through the seamless integration of initially segregated data regarding internal and external, social and non-social stimuli.

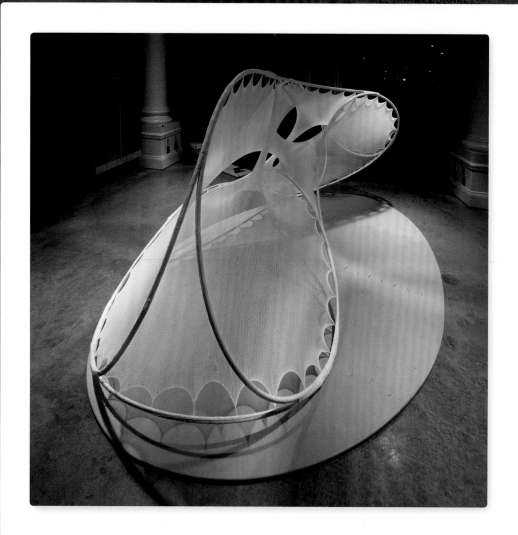

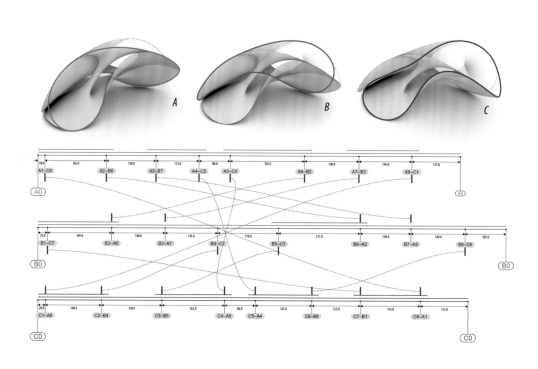

Sean Ahlquist,
Costanza Colombi,
Leah Ketcheson, Oliver
Popadich and Disha
Sharmin, Sensory
Playscape – textile
hybrid structure,
Southern Illinois
University, Carbondale,
Illinois, 2016

The prototype here showcases advancements in the use of CNC knitting and curved laminated glass-fibre reinforced beams, enabling the structure to serve as a spatially dynamic climbable landscape while maintaining its lightweight and flexible characteristics.

Interventions for ASD

Autism is a neurodevelopmental disorder that involves global impairments in social skills and in verbal and nonverbal communication, as well as the presence of stereotyped patterns of behaviour and interests. Epidemiological reports indicate that the number of children diagnosed with autism spectrum disorders is rising, currently affecting approximately 1 in 68 children in the US.[6]

Therapeutic intervention programmes such as applied behaviour analysis (ABA) for children with ASD have successfully targeted many different skills such as language and communication acquisition, academic, adaptive and social competence. But despite evidence that motor skills are specifically affected in ASD, attempts to acutely target this domain are rare in the clinical research arena. By including the design of an environment and the transformable nature of its spatiality, a therapeutic approach, as a result, embeds movement and attends to particular motor skills as a part of any mode of interaction.

In 2001, the US National Research Council named motor skills as one of eight domains to be targeted in the educational curriculum for children with ASD from birth through to eight years of age. Current research supports that movement abnormalities and early motor delays are among the earliest indicators of an eventual ASD diagnosis.[7] However, to date there remain very few interventions targeting movement behaviour as a primary outcome. In one such study, the effectiveness of a movement skill intervention was examined following an early and intensive eight-week-long motor-based programme for preschoolers aged between four and six.[8] The experimental group achieved a significant gain in fundamental motor skills and social skills following the intervention. This efficacy, of an intervention targeting motor outcomes while examining the effect on secondary domains, established the groundwork for the design of the environment, modes of interactions and means of assessment for the Sensory Surface and Playscape prototypes.

Movement, Social Behaviour and Dynamic Systems Theory

The concepts, therapies and prototypes explored in the ongoing multidisciplinary research at Michigan are grounded in a developmental theoretical framework known as dynamic systems theory (DST). Within DST, behaviour is believed to be a reflection of a complex and heterarchical interaction of multiple systems, where changes that emerge are often nonlinear.[9] The application of DST to movement is pivotal to the development of a multisensory architecture.

Within motor activity, both context and task drive the experience of new patterns of behaviour. The Sensory Surface and Playscape prototypes allow for new patterns to emerge through a range of variables in physical, visual and auditory sensation, all in continual transformation. Each child may repeatedly practise scaling up and down patterns of movement, such as applying pressure to the textile surfaces or moving through the spatial environment. Yet despite the repeated interaction, there exists enough variability for the environment to remain salient to the child while also producing, refining and generalising fine and gross motor changes.

Intrinsic dynamics within DST are the result of the personal history each child brings to a new task. Since children with ASD experience a wide profile of motor planning issues, the range of intrinsic dynamics was carefully considered in the creation of the Surface and Playscape prototypes so that the means of sensorial interaction can be tempered to a pace that best suits each child.

The perspective that impairments in one domain will affect the other has its grounding in a DST framework. Current research supports that children who experience a restricted selection of movement skills will have fewer opportunities for social exchanges with peers and lower levels of physical activity.[10] By creating opportunities to explore and refine new patterns of motor behaviour, the outcomes therefore have the potential to create a cascading effect. More explicitly, by increasing motor skills, participants may be more likely to experience health-enhancing physical activity and have more social opportunities with peers.

Sean Ahlquist,
Costanza Colombi,
Leah Ketcheson,
Oliver Popadich
and Disha Sharmin,
Sensory Playscape –
StretchSWARM prototype,
Taubman College of
Architecture and Urban
Planning, University
of Michigan, Ann Arbor,
Michigan, 2016

The bending-active components of the Sensory Playscape prototype are a multi-hierarchical system. Individual glass-fibre reinforced polymer rods are bundled into curved laminated beams, which are interconnected to form the overall rod geometry.

Sensory Playscapes

Tactile experience and patterns of movement are the primary design drivers in the Sensory Surface and Playscape prototypes, synthesising the research discussed here from the domains of architecture, psychiatry and kinesiology. Particularly with the Sensory Playscape prototype, the variegated nature of elasticity and spatial organisation defines the multisensory responsiveness at multiple scales. The architecture elicits three primary modes of interaction. First, physical exploration, or gross motor movement, is driven by the seamless interconnection of contoured surficial and volumetric geometries. Second, responsiveness to fine motor movements exists in the elastic forgiveness of the knitted textile, a consequence of yarn quality, stitch structure and the distribution of tensile forces. This is expressed in the balance of stretch and resistance at the touch of the hand, or in the encompassing contact between body and textile within the volumetric spaces. Lastly, movement and tactile sensation are augmented with visual and auditory feedback. In the case of dysfunctional processing of tactile stimulation, the multisensory feedback seeks to magnify and positively reinforce specific actions.

A textile hybrid system generates form via the structural equilibrium of tensile form-active surfaces and linear boundary elements stiffened through their configuration into curved geometries, forming a bending-active state.[11] In the research on textile hybrid structures taking place at the University of Michigan, the primary components are large-scale seamless CNC-knitted textiles and glass-fibre reinforced polymer rods laminated into curved beams. Both facets represent a second generation of development for the structural logic of textile hybrid systems, which is exemplified in the Sensory Playscape prototype. A typically self-stable system is thus transformed into one that can withstand significant and dynamic external loads.[12]

For both the Sensory Playscape and Sensory Surface prototypes, interactivity with the textile surfaces is enabled through the use of depth-mapping data from a Microsoft Kinect, providing a valuable separation between the hardware and the media for interaction. A contouring algorithm is utilised to measure touch and pressure with any configuration of flat, contoured and layered geometries. Location and depth of touch are identified and tracked, subsequently triggering the transformation of visuals projected onto the textiles and the choreography of the sonic experience of space. Two versions of such an interface have been developed using Unity: StretchCOLOR, where the user generates colours based on the amount of pressure applied to the surface, and StretchSWARM, where the flocking of objects is manipulated by interactions with the surface. The modes of interaction are all interchangeable, between the software and physical structures, a key capacity in evolving the nature of multisensory responsiveness as research progresses through the pilot study phase.

Tensile meshes simulated in springFORM, a Java-based form-finding software developed by Sean Ahlquist, are translated into data for CNC knitting. The topology uniquely comprises interconnected four-sided and cylindrical meshes in order to more intricately control the forms and relate them to strategies for CNC knitting.

Interaction with the textile hybrid structure is captured through three components as a part of a bespoke software developed in Unity: (1) a sensing component identifying location of touch and depth of interaction; (2) an interface component defining the visual and auditory feedback; and (3) a diagnostic component producing data for therapists to measure the interactions during each child's session.

Location and depth of touch are identified and tracked, subsequently triggering the transformation of visuals projected onto the textiles and the choreography of the sonic experience of space.

MESH TOPOLOGIES

SCHEMATIC FOR CNC KNITTING LOGIC

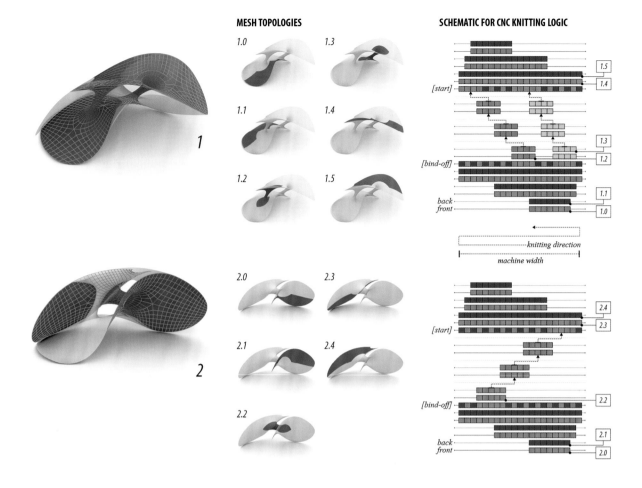

1

1.0 1.3
1.1 1.4
1.2 1.5

[start]

[bind-off]

back
front

1.5
1.4
1.3
1.2
1.1
1.0

knitting direction

machine width

2

2.0 2.3
2.1 2.4
2.2

[start]

[bind-off]

back
front

2.4
2.3
2.2
2.1
2.0

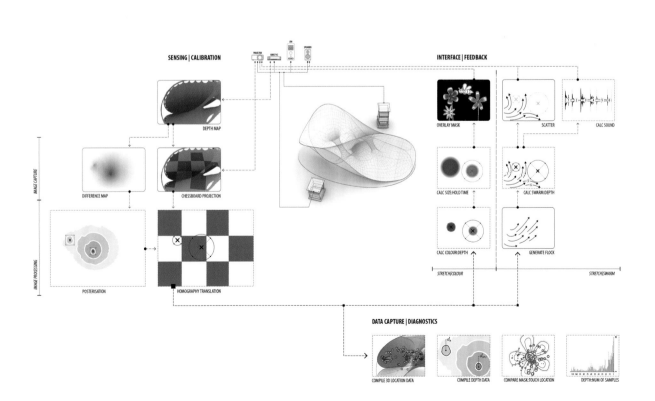

SENSING | CALIBRATION

INTERFACE | FEEDBACK

DEPTH MAP

DIFFERENCE MAP

CHESSBOARD PROJECTION

POSTERISATION

HOMOGRAPHY TRANSLATION

OVERLAY MASK

SCATTER

CALC SOUND

CALC SIZE:HOLD TIME

CALC SWARM:DEPTH

CALC COLOUR:DEPTH

GENERATE FLOCK

IMAGE CAPTURE

IMAGE PROCESSING

STRETCH|COLOUR

STRETCH|SWARM

DATA CAPTURE | DIAGNOSTICS

COMPILE 3D LOCATION DATA

COMPILE DEPTH DATA

COMPARE MASK:TOUCH LOCATION

DEPTH:NUM OF SAMPLES

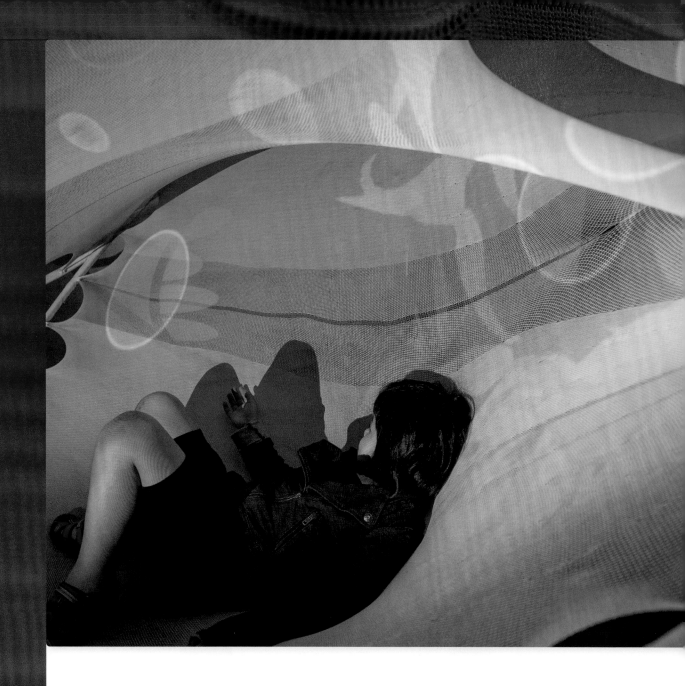

The multidisciplinary research discussed here requires the architecture of the prototypes to be defined as the embodiment of technology, environments, physical engagement and social function.

The Role of Multisensory Architectures

A hallmark of autism is the highly individualistic nature of each person's set of challenges – unique combinations and magnitudes of social, communicative and behavioural issues. While general assessments are often made, a specific relationship between behaviour and environment is difficult to extrapolate from individual to individual. The multidisciplinary research discussed here requires the architecture of the prototypes to be defined as the embodiment of technology, environments, physical engagement and social function. When empowering the individual to actively instrumentalise each nuance of such an architecture, a means for exploration, discovery and examination emerges. Applying these concepts to the interplay of environment, health and wellbeing is therefore captured not in the design of specific parameters, but rather in the capacity of those that engage it to specify the architecture.

The architecture as a whole itself acts as a communicative device. It serves as an extension and magnifier of the expressive and physical behaviours of the children. Physical movement is reinforced by an alteration of the geometry, which is reinforced by a dynamic visual. Movement of the visual is reinforced by the activation of sound. This generates a medium to observe, depict and document an individual's sensorial preferences, one that forms a state of regulated function, and ultimately intends to engender a confidence for social play. In forming patterns of sensory-reinforced social interaction, the architecture serves as the method by which the skill is generalised. The genesis of forming extensible patterns of behaviour emerges from this comprehensive view of architecture, as sensorial technologies that are engaging, transformable and multivalent, rather than engrossing, deterministic and repetitive. ⌀

Notes
1. Sean Ahlquist and Achim Menges, 'Materiality and Computational Design', in Mitra Kanaani and Dak Kopec (eds), *The Routledge Companion for Architecture Design and Practice*, Routledge (New York), 2016, p 164.
2. Joseph E Spradlin and Nancy Brady, 'Early Childhood Autism and Stimulus Control', in Patrick M Ghezzi, W Larry Williams and James E Carr (eds), *Autism: Behavior Analytic Perspectives*, Context Press (Reno, NV), 1999, pp 49–65.
3. Sally J Rogers, Susan Hepburn and Elizabeth Wehner, 'Parent Reports of Sensory Symptoms in Toddlers with Autism and those with Other Developmental Disorders', *Journal of Autism and Developmental Disorders*, 33, 2003, pp 631–42.
4. Jennifer Foss-Feig, Jessica Heacock and Carissa Cascio, 'Tactile Responsiveness Patterns and their Association with Core Features in Autism Spectrum Disorders', *Research in Autism Spectrum Disorders*, 6, 2012, p 337.
5. Ole I Lovaas and Tristram Smith, 'Early and Intensive Behavioral Intervention in Autism', in Alan E Kazdin and John R Weisz (eds), *Evidence-based Psychotherapies for Children and Adolescents*, Guilford Press (New York), 2003, pp 325–40.
6. Jon Baio, 'Prevalence of Autism Spectrum Disorder Among Children Aged 8 Years: Autism and Developmental Disabilities Monitoring Network, 11 Sites, United States, 2010', *Morbidity and Mortality Weekly Report*, 63 (2), 2014, pp 1–21.
7. Joanne E Flanagan et al, 'Head Lag in Infants at Risk for Autism: A Preliminary Study', *American Journal of Occupational Therapy*, 66, 2012, pp 577–85.
8. Leah Ketcheson, Janet Hauck and Dale Ulrich, 'The Effect of Early Motor Skill Intervention on Motor Skills, Level of Physical Activity, and Socialization in Young Children with Autism Spectrum Disorder: A Pilot Study', *Autism*, 26 June 2016.
9. Esther Thelen and Linda Smith, *Dynamic Systems Theories: Handbook of Child Psychology*, John Wiley & Sons (New York), 1998, p 258.
10. Megan Macdonald, Catherine Lord and Dale Ulrich, 'Motor Skills and Calibrated Autism Severity in Young Children with Autism Spectrum Disorder', *Adapted Physical Activity Quarterly*, 31(2), 2014, pp 95–105.
11. Sean Ahlquist, 'Social Sensory Architectures: Articulating Textile Hybrid Structures for Multi-sensory Responsiveness and Collaborative Play', in Lonn Combs and Chris Perry (eds), *Proceedings of ACADIA 2015: Computational Ecologies – Design in the Anthropocene*, Vol 2, Association for Computer Aided Design in Architecture (ACADIA), 2015, pp 262–73.
12. Sean Ahlquist and Julian Lienhard, 'Extending Geometric and Structural Capacities for Textile Hybrid Structures with Laminated GFRP Beams and CNC Knitting', in IASS 2016 (forthcoming).

Sean Ahlquist,
Costanza Colombi,
Leah Ketcheson,
Oliver Popadich
and Disha Sharmin,
Sensory Playscape
– StretchSWARM
prototype,
HandsOn Museum,
Ann Arbor,
Michigan,
2016

During the event at the HandsOn Museum, some children preferred submersing themselves within the structure as a form of interacting with the textiles and visual projections.

Stephen Verderber

Deploying the tent component
over a mobile triage/
surgical truck in Tunisia,
North Africa in the Second
World War,
1944

These were proven effective as first-
response medical aid stations along the
front lines in the desert.

Architects as First Responders

Portable Healthcare Architecture in a Climate-Altered World

In both developed and developing countries, medical emergencies caused by the effects of climate change, earthquakes, war or terrorism can wreak havoc with healthcare infrastructure. Where hospitals are lacking, or existing ones are overburdened or put out of action, prefabricated transportable solutions are indispensable for rebuilding afflicted communities. **Stephen Verderber** – a current Professor at the University of Toronto and former Professor in the Graduate Program in Architecture + Health at Clemson University in South Carolina – gives examples of the types of systems that exist, and highlights key considerations to be taken into account by those involved in their design.

Highly challenging global events are upending the rhythms of everyday life. Earthquakes, intense hurricanes and typhoons, flooding, famine, tsunamis, wars and acts of terrorism, ethnic strife, and geopolitical conflicts waged over dwindling natural resources are becoming commonplace. In developed and developing regions alike, tens of millions of people are at increased risk. The Intergovernmental Panel on Climate Change (IPCC) confirms that our planet is experiencing accelerated climate change at a rate significantly faster than previously anticipated.[1] In Bangladesh in 2011 alone, more than 60,000 internally displaced persons (IDPs) became permanently homeless due to rising seas and subsequent widespread inland flooding that overwhelmed the region's already fragile infrastructure.[2] By 2050, it is predicted that nearly 80 per cent of the world's population will reside in coastal zones. This, coupled with the unprecedented ramifications of global climate change, constitutes an ideal recipe for innumerable disasters in the years ahead.[3]

That said, the need exists for the rapid deployment of healthcare infrastructure to medically underserved disaster strike zones: mobile facilities able to be transited, erected and operationalised under very challenging timeframes. In this regard – with more individuals and places than ever susceptible to life-threatening outcomes of wider scope, intensity and duration – the World Health Organization (WHO) is calling for architectural research and development to invent innovative, sustainable, resilient responses to these adverse global events.

Conventional, fixed-site hospitals certainly serve a critical role in such situations, although they themselves are susceptible to fails because they are 'sitting ducks', so to speak.[4] Permanently sited institutions are at risk of shutdown for weeks if not months, as occurred in the aftermath of Hurricane Katrina in New Orleans in 2005.[5] Transportable clinics, alternatively, offer a flexible counterpoint to conventional brick-and-mortar hospitals and clinics: they are able to be expeditiously deployed via airlift, ship, rail, roadway or multi-modal methods and have already proven their efficacy for more than a century. They have ably served in times of war, including the truck-based triage units deployed by Allied forces in North Africa in the Second World War. They provide first-response medical support in post-disaster humanitarian aid efforts, such as in the aftermath of the Haitian (2010) and Ecuadorian (2016) earthquakes. Traditionally, the vast majority of portable buildings for healthcare have emanated from military organisations, whereas a smaller percentage of privately financed portables for health are typically commissioned by non-governmental organisations (NGOs). Rapid response must be of utmost priority, to enable the expeditious transiting of the system/building and then its quick assembly on site. Generally, three types of mobile prefab systems for health applications exist: redeployable health centres (RHCs), redeployable trauma centres (RTCs) and permanent site modular installations (PMIs).

Five Variants: Transportables for Health

Within this typology, five variants are most promising at this time. The first of these – tent-based and pneumatic structures – are the most prevalent sort in use globally. Variations on the ancient tent and yurt have inspired most systems of this type in current use. Tents are lightweight, versatile, adaptable to diverse cultural and occupant needs, and responsive to topographically challenging terrain and many climatological contexts. Tent-based systems have evolved significantly in recent years, including the emergence of modular pneumatic systems. The majority of tent and pneumatic systems for health applications are commissioned by military organisations for deployment to combat theatres, such as the DEPMEDS (deployable medical units) used by the US Army in Iraq from Operation Desert Storm in 1991 until the end of the Iraq War in 2013. However, with the parallel dramatic increase in the occurrence of global disasters, these systems have taken on a more prominent role than ever before in humanitarian aid missions.

The second most prevalent type in current use is the vehicular nomadic unit. These RHCs and RTCs are prefabricated modules with additional interior componentry incorporated. Integral units (a single mobile entity) and two-element truck/trailer configurations predominate. The mobile field hospital proposed by a US architectural firm for the Moroccan Ministry of Health in 2010 consisted of a 48-bed inpatient hospital housed in numerous two-element modular units. Here, the MONARCH Corporation teamed with architects Hord Coplan Macht, of Baltimore, Maryland, to develop a full-scale nomadic, redeployable field hospital. This RHC/RTC inpatient installation is scalable up to 58 vehicular units, with some functioning as satellites transiting to and from nearby yet remote sites and then docking at the 'mothership' by night – without compromising intra-module connectivity.

Third, intermodal containerised systems have become the modular preferred choice for many healthcare organisations due to high structural strength and proven resilience in difficult transiting conditions across long distances. Containerised systems perform particularly well in this regard and can be close-packed during transit. They are typically custom-built, but some are based on adapted standardised shipping containers.[6] In the aftermath of the earthquake in Haiti, a US-based NGO, Care 2 Communities (C2C; formerly known as Containers 2 Clinics), commissioned three women's-health outpatient clinics. Generic containers provided the blank canvas for STANTEC/Stack Design's response. The installation consisted of three modules sited in close proximity to one another, creating an open-air courtyard at the centre. This space serves as the 'waiting room': a wooden deck with moveable chairs beneath a canvas roof that shields patients from the intense sun and frequent tropical downpours.

STANTEC/Stack Design,
C2C Women's Health Clinic,
Port-au-Prince,
Haiti,
2011

This unit was adapted from standard ISO (International Organization for Standardization) containers. Later units were custom-built to the client's detailed performance specifications.

Hord Coplan Macht with MONARCH
Corporation, Mobile field hospital
developed for the Moroccan Ministry
of Health, 2010

Essentially a kit-of-parts, various combinations
of modules are reconfigurable as needs change.
Subsets of satellite units are able to un-dock and
travel to local villages, returning to re-dock at
night.

Fourth, flat-packs and pop-up systems consist of kit-of-parts assemblies shipped in standardised intermodal containers or specially designed containers. Upon arrival at the site of deployment, contents are removed and assembled. After this, the modules used strictly in transiting are storable on site or useable for ancillary functions, such as medications, clinical supplies, and equipment. Pop-ups are able to function as PMIs or RHCs, and can be effective rapid-response interventions in medically underserved communities in either routine everyday or post-disaster scenarios. Here, an existing structure functions as the host, with one or more pop-up modules installed within it. The possibilities for this type of intervention were recently explored in a research project within the Graduate Program in Architecture + Health at Clemson University in South Carolina (USA). Charleston, South Carolina and New Orleans, Louisiana were selected as the host cities. In these two communities, both situated in low-lying coastal regions, the adverse impacts of hurricanes and attendant tidal surge flooding are a constant threat. Both urban areas are predominately low-lying, with historical neighbourhoods containing many suitable host structures, heritage or otherwise, including neighbourhood churches, schools and their gymnasiums, and vacant commercial storefronts. Nineteen host structures were subsequently pre-tested for suitability via proposals to insert, in some hosts, an emergency triage unit, and in other hosts, a primary care clinic. It was learned that both cities would benefit from pop-up interventions in host structures because they could help empower residents to return confidently to their neighbourhood sooner than would probably be the case otherwise. This is because, in both cities, most (if not all) local brick-and-mortar hospitals would probably remain offline for weeks (if not months). In one proposed intervention in Charleston, a historical African-American congregational church is adapted into a host to a pop-up primary care RHC.

The fifth variant – hybrid portable systems – are composite and at times eclectic assemblies. This variant can consist of all three types (RHC/RTC/PMI) on a single site, synthesising the strongest attributes of intermodal containerised systems and tent- and mobile unit-based systems. When integrated, a tent or pneumatically activated membrane system, combined with modular containers, can afford a broad scope of aesthetic and functional performance possibilities. Their hybridity utilises offsite prefabrication construction methods with on-site manual construction assistance performed by local relief aid workers. Internal functions are distributed across 'hard' (container) and 'soft' (tent) portions of the total system. One example, the unbuilt SmartPOD (2013) proposal, developed at Clemson University in 2013, is a hybrid capable of operating remotely or tethered to a stationary medical centre. It is inspired by the aforementioned US portable infirmaries deployed in the Middle East. The undercarriage is a 12-metre-long (40-foot) custom-built module. Upon arrival, following container positioning, structural masts are erected followed by attachment of double-curvature tents stabilised by means of tension cables. The deployment illustrated is proposed for Washington, DC in the aftermath of a bioterrorist attack on the US Capitol.

George Hughes with Stephen Verderber
(Clemson University Graduate Program
in Architecture + Health), Pop-up
modular installation proposal
for Church of Christ, Charleston,
South Carolina, 2013

Plan and exterior view. This church has been a
landmark in the African-American community
in Charleston for over a century.

Key:

C1-C6	behavioral health consultation*	13	medications
E1-E6	examination room*	14	subwaiting
I1-I4	patient intake*	15	nutrition
1	patient sign-in	16	director
2	waiting area	17	immunisations
3	laboratory	18	physicians
4	medications	19	biohazardous waste
5	office	20	health education/ conference
6	clerical: work zone	21	staff kitchen
7	medical records	22	housekeeping/janitor
8	staff restroom	23	storeroom
9	men's restroom	24	volunteers
10	women's restroom	25	nursing
11	patient restroom	26	TB/STD
12	environmental health		

*   The number of rooms varies across the sites as a
function of its installation site footprint.

With regards to off-site prefabrication, inventive internal planning and manufacture of all modular parts is absolutely essential. It is often said, 'First and foremost, honour the matchline,' as this refers to the need for tight, precise connections and fittings between all componentry. Interior work and treatment zones need to optimalise the caregiver's ability to perform at the highest level. System-wide concerns include siting, aesthetics, internal ambiance, the installation's rapid identification, day or night, along with the provision of high-level air quality, natural daylight, artificial illumination, functional spatial adjacencies, ceiling configuration options, and provisions for furnishings and equipment. Some installations in current use, such as the field hospital owned by the Canadian Red Cross, arrive in a relatively self-sufficient state, complete with earth-moving devices, forklifts and modular power generation packages. As for siting concerns, football pitches, car parks, urban streets, parks and open fields are sought after. A system should be designed for autonomous operations or in tandem with a fixed-site hospital, as was the case with the BLU-MED portable facility deployed to Haiti in the aftermath of the 2010 earthquake. Flat-pack componentry typically can yield a more efficient use of containerisation space while en route, although the system then must be fully assembled on site. In systems based on variants of customised shipping containers, modules can be plugged together, resulting in a rigid, monolithic platform not unlike in the assembly of an automobile. Final assembly on site typically takes place by local workers under the guidance of trained personnel with (presumably) prior experience.

Section depicting the inner membrane of a typical module, with the outer structure aperture housing medical gases and related support infrastructure.

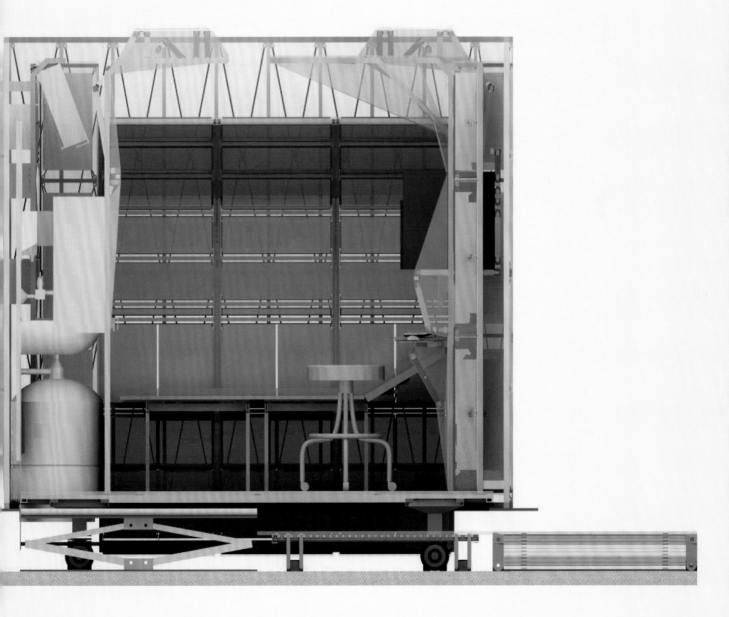

George Hughes with Stephen Verderber
(Clemson University Graduate Program in Architecture + Health),
SmartPOD portable hospital,
2013

Hybrid system comprised of containers, flat-pack panels and tents that provide substantial natural ventilation and daylight. This installation was proposed for deployment on Pennsylvania Avenue in Washington DC in the immediate aftermath of a bioterrorist attack.

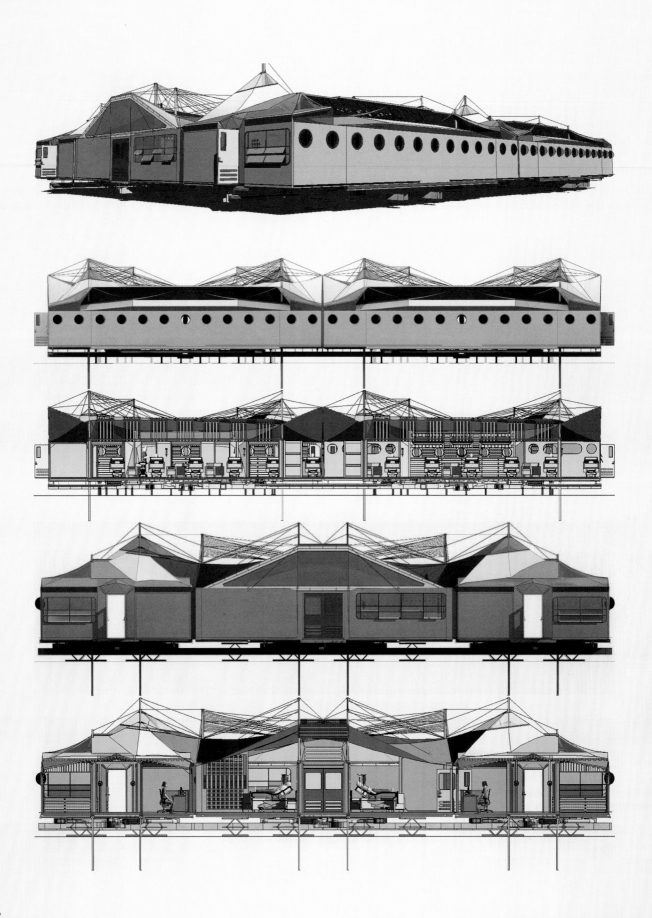

Sustainable Healthcare Architecture and Portability

Is the underwhelming current reputation of the architect as a first responder wholly justified? Probably so. But before this can change for the better, a genuine attitude of public service, outreach, empathy and compassion for the plight of persons and places in need must exist. Off-site-built prefab precursors in housing and other building types warrant further research so that lessons can be learned and strengths, shortcomings and risk factors identified *a priori*. A working knowledge of sustainable off-site prefab processes must be carefully developed, including system tectonics, environmental support systems, transiting determinants, commissioning and decommissioning processes, daily functional performance and midstream retrofitting – while concurrently respecting the Vitruvian principles of architecture's provision of commodity, firmness and delight.[7] As for the sponsor/client, including NGOs, ministries of health, and policy specialists, it behooves all to embrace, far more than occurs now, the vast collaborative potential of architecture, engineering and industrial design to improve how things are done at present.

Transportable architecture for health can contribute to a community's bounce-back resiliency, its future sustainability, and therefore its reconstituted, collective social capital. Albeit, shattered social networks are very challenging to reconstitute. The presence of a portable prefab clinic can symbolise that it is safe, it is OK to return. This alone greatly aids in fostering reaffirmative place-reattachment behaviours, behaviours prerequisite to effective community rebuilding. A portable structure for health simultaneously fosters ecological sustainability for the way it is built, alone, versus, by comparison, carbon-neutral advancements in fixed-site architecture for health that are often slow to be adopted, with sustainability innovations occurring, randomly, in a series of fits and starts. The examples discussed above seek to attain the most efficient use of construction materials and to recycle material waste. Energy consumption is measurable, including mechanical, electrical, plumbing systems and daily maintenance expenses – with the aim of infusing clean energy sources (solar, wind) and maximising geographic and climatological functional range as well as an installation's ecological lightness. Beyond this, as inferred above, a portable, nomadic healthcare facility can foster health-promotion and community rebuilding by simply arriving at the pre- or post-disaster site in a timely manner. The ability to administer first-response triage, the testing of water samples, immunisations and chemical agent decontamination in addition to minor surgical procedures, is of indispensible value to caregivers and victims alike.

For the discipline of architecture, and particularly for the architectural historian, it continues to remain a challenge to properly place portable buildings within broader theory-based discursive streams of inquiry and analysis. Despite this ever-present conundrum, progressive experimentation continues to be absolutely essential if architects and allied designers are to achieve measurable success in meeting the global need for first-response, sustainable architecture of this type. ᴆ

BLU-MED Response Systems
with Alaska Structures,
BLU-MED tent system,
Haitian field deployment,
2010

Tent systems continue to be preferred by many first-response aid organisations for their lightness and ability to be erected locally by unskilled volunteers under the direction of trained personnel. The BLU-MED system is fabricated with lightweight aluminium frames for expeditious assembly.

Notes
1. Intergovernmental Panel on Climate Change, *Fifth Assessment Report: Climate Change 2014 – Impacts, Adaptation, and Vulnerability*, Cambridge University Press (Cambridge), 2014: www.ipcc.ch/report/ar5/wg2/.
2. Donald R Prothero, *Catastrophes!: Earthquakes, Tsunamis, Tornadoes and Other Earth-Shattering Disasters*, Johns Hopkins University Press (Baltimore, MD), 2011.
3. Brian Kahn, 'Floods May Cost Coastal Cities $60 Billion a Year by 2050', *ClimateCentral.org*, 18 August 2013: www.climatecentral.org/news/floods-may-cost-coastal-cities-60-billion-annually-by-2050-16356.
4. Crystal Franco, Eric Toner, Richard Waldhorn, Beth Maldin, Tara O'Toole and Thomas V Inglesby, 'Systemic Collapse: Medical Care in the Aftermath of Hurricane Katrina', *Biosecurity and Bioterrorism*, 4(2), 2006, pp 135–46: http://online.liebertpub.com/doi/pdfplus/10.bsp.2006.4.135.html.
5. Stephen Verderber, 'Evidence-Based Design for Healthcare in Post-Katrina New Orleans: Current Dilemmas', *Health Environments Research and Design Journal*, 1(2), 2008, pp 71–9.
6. Stephen Verderber, 'Redeployable Trauma Centers for Post-Disaster Response', *World Health Design*, 5(3), October 2012, pp 56–61.
7. Stephen Verderber, *Innovations in Transportable Healthcare Architecture*, Routledge (London), 2016.

Giuseppe Boscherini

A Sense of Coherence
Supporting the Healing Process

Can patient recovery be actively aided by a well-designed hospital setting? The evidence is that it can. Drawing on sociologist Aaron Antonovsky's concept of salutogenesis, architect, industrial and interior designer **Giuseppe Boscherini** argues that an environment which balances calming reassurance with constructive stimulation can help instil the positive mindset that people need in order to overcome illness. Referring to buildings by practices he has worked for, and a student project he has led, he shows how light, sound, texture and colour can all contribute to health-giving architecture.

A few years ago I spent a week in hospital undergoing surgery. A print hanging on the wall opposite my bed, intended to uplift the decor, haunted my nights. My dazed mind, inebriated by anaesthetics, was hallucinating about its graphic details. In a state of sedated stupor I asked myself: Can the design of a restorative environment stimulate patient recovery by instilling a positive mindset?

As architects and interior designers we intuitively sense that space and mood are connected. This is supported by substantive evidence linking pain thresholds and speed of recovery to lighting and colour.[1]

Design Heals

Professor Alan Dilani of the International Academy for Design and Health argues that implementing designs that are salutogenic, which focus on factors that keep us well, can speed up the recovery of health.[2] While this stands to reason, much of healthcare architecture is governed by strictly clinical standards; to paraphrase Le Corbusier, the hospital is often presented as 'a machine for healing', the technological design aspects of which help to reinforce the perception among patients that their ailments are being treated in a scientific manner.[3] By contrast, the aim of psychosocially supportive design is to stimulate the mind in order to induce a sense of wellbeing.

The World Health Organization defines health as 'a state of complete physical, mental and social wellbeing and not merely the absence of disease or infirmity'.[4] Aaron Antonovsky, who coined the term 'salutogenesis' – from the Latin *salus* meaning health, and the Greek *genesis* for origin – believed that there is an important relationship between the physical environment and an individual's sense of coherence.[5] We understand this commonly as 'keeping it together' in the face of adversity, and it manifests itself, when facing serious health challenges, through manageability: the availability of resources and a supportive social network; comprehensibility, intended as a comforting backdrop that offers order and familiarity; and meaningfulness, understood as the inspiring realisation that there are important 'phenomena' in life and nature.[6]

It follows that the ideal spatial framework for salutogenic design translates into three key components: welcoming spaces for meeting and social exchange; familiar spaces for orientation and reassurance; and quiet spaces for meditation and restoration.

A Sensory Experience

IBI Group's design for a dementia care unit for the Northamptonshire Healthcare NHS Foundation Trust in 2011 demonstrates that an environment that reinforces confidence in the self-healing process is one that balances the need for calm and reassurance with that for constructive stimulation of the senses.

On the one hand, familiarity is important as it breeds self-confidence and directly supports a patient's sense of coherence.[7] In spatial terms, recollecting and recognising are about making crucial information obvious, concealing the unnecessary and offering multiple clues; in this sense the building becomes a roadmap to recovery.

IBI Group,
Forest Centre dementia unit,
St Mary's Hospital,
Kettering,
Northamptonshire,
2011

Using a selection of familiar
objects and images in a variety
of connected settings triggers
memory and aids orientation.

On the other hand, stimulus is beneficial as it stirs emotions and triggers neurological activity. In spatial terms, the environment should ideally offer a variety of spaces, in size and character, internal and external, all benefitting from good-quality air and light. Paradoxically, indoor environmental quality of therapeutic architecture is often determined by engineering standards, rather than by health criteria.

IBI Group advocates an understanding of how our senses interact with the physical environment when we are coping with illness.[8] In the context of dementia care, this translates into a design that caters for needs associated with all five senses, the most easily understood of which is sight. Artificial lighting and natural daylight have a positive effect on elderly people's ability to see and focus on objects, distinguish colours, judge distances and compensate for shadowing effects. Sound is a close second in terms of preventing competing noises through good sound insulation and absorption, inducing restorative sleep and better mood, while also enabling the enjoyment of (good) music, which is proven to be analgesic and to lower blood pressure and heart rate.

Smell and taste sensations go hand in hand in their ability to subtly awaken senses, helping to restore the pleasure associated with, say, flowers or fresh fruit. Floral and fruit fragrances have indeed been proven to lower blood pressure, slow down respiration, relax muscles and increase alertness. Finally, and perhaps not so obviously, a varied choice of textures can turn the sense of touch into both stimulus and soothing comfort.

Designing a sensory experience, whether it is calming or exciting, therefore means designing from the inside out; that is, from the responses that carers hope to elicit from their patients.

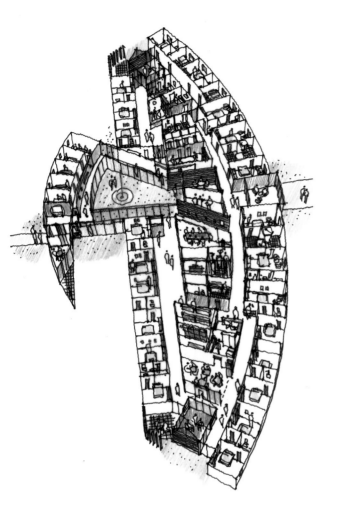

Exposure to bright morning
light has been shown to reduce
agitation among elderly patients
with dementia.

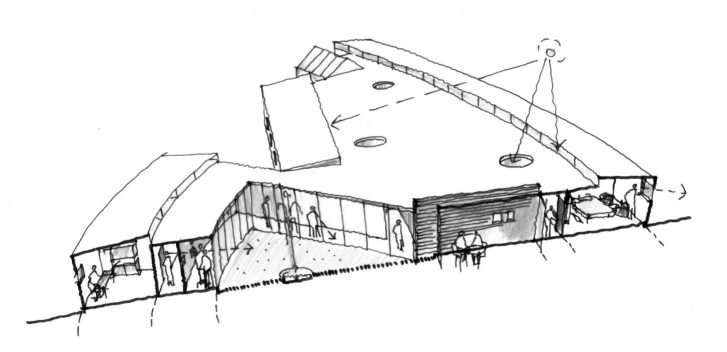

The Nature Connection

With the backdrop of impressive medical advances, to most the suggestion that real benefits may derive from merely 'being in a place' sounds deceiving. Yet there is no great secret at work in the positive impact of Maggie's cancer care centres (see the article by Maggie's cofounder Charles Jencks on pp 66–75 of this issue).[9] They are defined by positive qualities: light, space, openness, intimacy, views, and connection to nature – the opposite of a standard-issue hospital environment. In the words of the 'Maggie's Architecture and Landscape Brief', Maggie's Centres 'must look and feel joyous; they must have zest as well as calm'.[10]

The latest addition is the Maggie's Centre designed by Foster + Partners at the Christie Hospital in Manchester, which opened in April 2016. According to Norman Foster: 'Our aim in Manchester … was to create a building that is welcoming, friendly and without any of the institutional references of a hospital or health centre.'[11] The idea starts with a landscaped space, designed by Dan Pearson, around which patient care is organised. The location of the building allows morning and afternoon sunlight to penetrate private and social areas. The focus is on 'natural light, greenery and views … and an emphasis on the therapeutic qualities of nature and the outdoors'.[12]

Evidence from clinical trials shows that being outdoors positively impacts on circadian rhythms, blood pressure, attentiveness, verbal expression, restoration and behaviour. Maggie was herself a landscape designer, and her original blueprint for the centres placed great emphasis on the role of landscaped outdoor spaces in creating a place to promote communication, activity and positive mental health. Foster + Partners's centre aids familiarity and orientation through its domestic planning and feel, yet is also refreshing and stimulating in its relationship with daylight and nature.

Social to Private Progression

In 2016, the teaching staff at the KLC School of Design in London set their interior design diploma students a challenging brief devised to engage their creativity and critical thinking in the design of a hospital ward. The context was a project for the Royal Hospital for Neuro-disability (RHN). Founded in 1854 in Putney, southwest London, the RHN is the oldest and most respected independent hospital and medical charity in the UK. Its stated mission is 'to meet the needs of people with complex disabilities which have arisen from a profound brain injury'.[13]

The students were introduced from the outset to the notion of salutogenesis as the guiding principle of their design. Working as groups, they responded differently to the challenge, but all with great enthusiasm. The Horizon team, led by Sabine Gern, elected to design Draper's Ward in such a way as to empower personal choice and autonomy through, in her own words, 'enhancing quality of life for the individual by providing choice and strengthening connections'. The intent behind the ward design was that patients with neuro-disabilities should be able to personalise their space and retain independence for as long as possible. This was achieved in spatial terms through clearly expressing the transition from communal to individual spaces, providing interesting circulation routes, enhancing social contact by locating the interactive area at the ward's entrance, and designing bedrooms as 'sanctuaries' to reinforce personal identity.

Foster + Partners,
Maggie's Centre,
Christie Hospital,
Manchester,
UK,
2016

Access to outside spaces as well as views to a courtyard landscape create a beneficial connection with nature.

Sabine Gern/KLC
School of Design,
Draper's Ward,
Royal Hospital for
Neuro-disability,
London,
2016

The layout balances privacy, through bedrooms designed to help support patient autonomy, with interaction, by creating a feeling of hospitality that is non-institutional, pleasant and welcoming.

Office & staff	
Community	
Kitchen & eating	
Therapy	
Utility	
Bathroom	
Sleep	
Sensory	

Health-Promoting Lifestyle Centres

In 2011, the South African Department of Health funded an international design competition to build exemplar Health-Promoting Lifestyle Centres (HPLCs). Its purpose was to shift the country's health system towards a salutogenic model of health promotion, wellness education, preventative care and early intervention.[14] Design objectives included facilitating a sustainable lifestyle, supporting learning and enabling stress management.

IBI Group's competition entry explored a new model of sustainable healthcare architecture where HPLCs would interact with local communities by offering three types of spaces, symbolised by 'Hand', 'Mind' and 'Heart'. The Hand is a place of arrival, a busy place of trade and exchange, both cultural and commercial; the Mind is a place of welcome and a centre of information, offering comprehensibility; and the Heart is a place of assessment and medication, but also a retreat.

IBI Group,
Health-Promoting Lifestyle Centres,
Soweto,
Khayelitsha and KwaZulu-Natal,
South Africa,
2011

The courtyard is a building typology that represents shelter, retreat and focus and evokes feelings of spiritual relaxation and restoration.

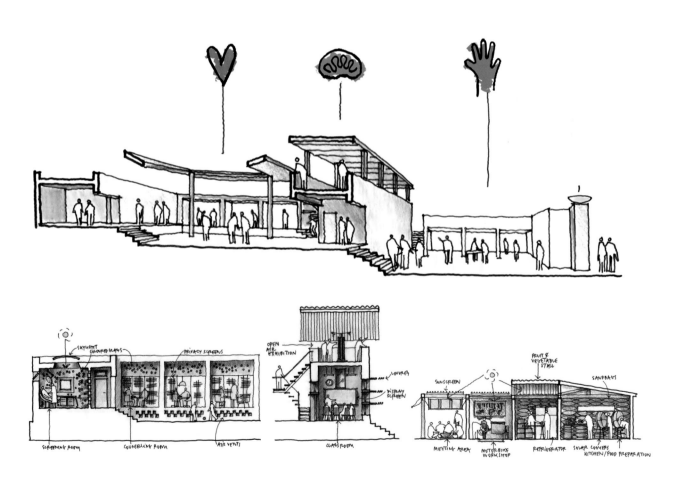

IBI Group,
Health-Promoting
Lifestyle Centres,
Soweto,
Khayelitsha and
KwaZulu-Natal,
South Africa,
2011

Architectural expression
may vary according to local
character, while sequence
of spaces and articulation of
volumes remain a constant
feature.

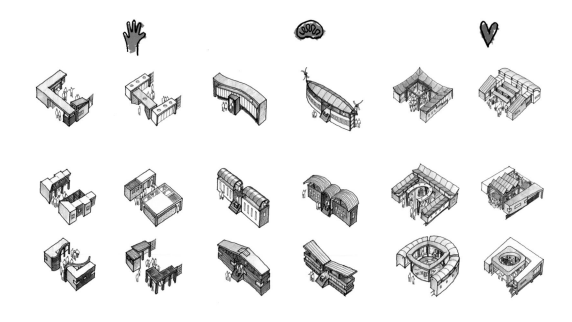

Self-awareness that promotes
health is also the basis for a
collective consciousness about
the environment that favours
local or reclaimed materials,
vernacular construction
techniques and sustainable
renewable technologies.

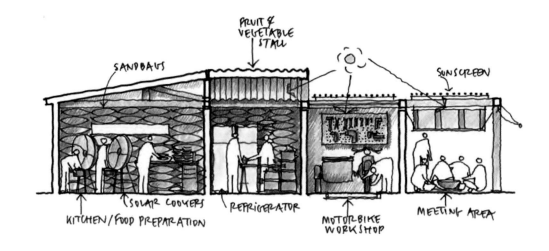

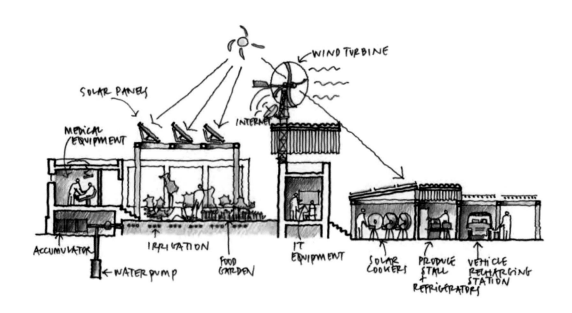

The three elements are organised around two courtyards linked by a journey of discovery, which begins with the public and familiar of the Hand courtyard, rising through the informative and educational of the Mind building, to the inspiring and nurturing of the Heart courtyard. The courtyard is a universal and historical feature of meditative and vernacular architecture from the traditional Tanzanian courthouse, through the Chinese merchant house to the Egyptian temple.

Customisation, achieved through a process of consultation, accommodates local community requirements and yields locally sustainable and relevant architectural typologies and health-promoting strategies. A sustainable approach informs both the construction and use of the HPLCs, promoting a sense of coherence with one's environment, understood across a broad range of interdependencies, with natural ecosystems and resources, with social community and clinical infrastructure, and importantly with family and carers.

Space as Sustainable Therapy

Much of the focus of contemporary medical practice is on supporting patients who strive to cope with their illness. Space can be an integral part of therapy when it provides a framework for living with a chronic condition. In this sense, a therapeutic environment that is truly sustainable is informed by thinking about health in its broadest sense, and by an understanding of sustained care in the community. Macmillan Cancer Support states that: 'Space, art and gardens are key in our most recent projects, to help people feel comfortable during treatment or palliative care.'[15]

A good restorative environment is well balanced, beautiful and reflective, using colour, texture, light and sound to overcome cognitive dissonance. It brings about a sense of coherence, at an individual and community level, when its design is based on an understanding of emotional as well as physical needs. As such it must act as a holistic care environment through supporting emotional, social, physical and mental wellbeing; enhancing involvement with family and carers by providing a sense of meaning and purpose; creating an open feel through connections with nature, daylight, air, time and seasons; and being legible and intuitively simple to navigate by offering natural orientation, familiarity and recognition. ⌂

Notes
1. Ruth Brent Tofle, Benyamin Schwarz, So-Yeon Yoon and Andrea Max-Royale, *Color In Healthcare Environments*, Coalition for Health Environments Research (CHER) (San Francisco, CA), 2004
2. Alan Dilani, 'Psychosocially Supportive Design: A Salutogenic Approach to the Design of the Physical Environment', SHB2009 – 1st International Conference on Sustainable Healthy Buildings, Seoul, 6 February 2009, pp 55–65.
3. Leslie Topp, 'An Architecture for Modern Nerves: Josef Hoffmann's Purkersdorf Sanatorium', *Journal of the Society of Architectural Historians*, 56 (4), 1997, pp 414–37.
4. 'Preamble to the Constitution of the World Health Organization as adopted by the International Health Conference', *Official Records of the World Health Organization*, No 2, 1946, p 100.
5. Aaron Antonovsky, *Unravelling the Mystery of Health*, Jossey-Bass (San Francisco), 1987.
6. Bengt Lindström and Monica Eriksson, *The Hitchhiker's Guide to Salutogenesis*, Folkhälsan (Helsinki), 2010.
7. Alan Dilani and Kathleen Armstrong, *The 'Salutogenic' Approach: Designing a Health-Promoting Hospital Environment*, PubMed (Bethesda, MD), 2008.
8. Lorraine Farrelly, ⌂ *Designing for the Third Age: Architecture Redefined for a Generation of 'Active Agers'*, March/April (no 2), 2014, pp 108–11.
9. See also Steve Rose, 'Maggie's Centres: Can Architecture Cure Cancer?', *The Guardian*, 6 May 2010: www.theguardian.com/artanddesign/2010/may/06/maggies-centres-cancer-architecture.
10. Maggie's Architecture and Landscape Brief: www.maggiescentres.org/media/uploads/publications/other-publications/Maggies_architecturalbrief_2015.pdf.
11. Amy Frearson, 'Norman Foster's Timber-framed Maggie's Centre Opens in his Home Town of Manchester', *Dezeen*, 27 April 2016: www.dezeen.com/2016/04/27/norman-foster-partners-maggies-centre-cancer-care-manchester-england/.
12. *Ibid.*
13. www.rhn.org.uk/what-makes-us-special/ethos/.
14. Nancy Coulson, 'Health Promotion in South Africa', *Health Systems Trust Update*, 53, 2000, p 3.
15. Macmillan Cancer Support: www.macmillan.org.uk/howwecanhelp/cancerenvironments/cancerenvironments.aspx.

The balance and spatial arrangement of therapeutic activities is a function of local needs understood through consultation. In the Khayelitsha township, the focus might be, for instance, on entrepreneurship, allowing the Hand to cater for rentable start-up shop units trading the produce of the Heart's community food garden.

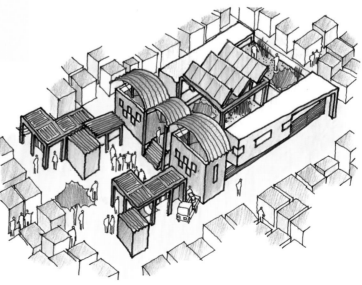

Designing for health and wellbeing can be a daunting task for architects, especially in the healthcare sector where there are countless complexities to resolve and restrictions to accommodate. Sophisticated programming and space-planning tools have been developed to address the clinical and technical aspects of healthcare design. These tools, however, do not begin to address the non-clinical yet fundamental components of the care facility – the spaces 'in-between'. These are the spaces where we find ourselves as we search for entries and exits, walk from department to department, and wait, vulnerably, with our loved ones. They are, too often, entirely unsatisfactory, embittering and often polluting the care experience. They tend to be isolated within the depths of a building, removed from natural light, views to nature and access to the outdoors. Yet it is the quality, character and configuration of these spaces that can make or break our healthcare experience.

As extensions of our public realm, these in-between spaces carry enormous potential to enhance the care environment, offering critical opportunities to make it not only tolerable, but also pleasant for those whose wellbeing is compromised, as well as the families and staff who support them. At Montgomery Sisam Architects, we relish the opportunity to elevate non-clinical spaces to the best they can possibly be, even if this necessitates disrupting and rethinking the status quo in healthcare planning. This article focuses on the evolution of the practice's thinking about non-clinical spaces in healthcare design, and the fundamental role of in-between spaces in framing the firm's approach.

The Search for an Alternative Paradigm in Healthcare Design
When the practice was first started in Toronto in the late 1970s, we were disillusioned with the stale, heavy-handed modernism of the time, especially in designs for institutional buildings. Cars were overrunning cities and institutions were turning in on themselves, becoming isolated and removed from their communities. Healthcare planning in particular had become more rationalised, and human dignity an afterthought. We believed, however, that through design we could make a tangible contribution to people's health and wellbeing.

As a student on a travelling scholarship in the late 1960s, I had chosen to explore small, unassuming towns in Ireland, France and Spain rather than the renowned European works of pedigreed architects. There I witnessed for myself what life was like in seemingly timeless settings, supporting the wellbeing of countless generations of inhabitants. At Montgomery Sisam, we aspired to make similar places that honoured the comforts and pleasures of everyday life, and continued to search for inspiration wherever we could find it. Jane Jacobs had recently moved to Toronto and her *Life and Death of Great American Cities* (1961)[1] fostered our respect for the street and the buildings that support it, while Gordon Cullen's spare, insightful drawings in his book *The Concise Townscape* (1961)[2] renewed our appreciation for the formal variation and texture of urban spaces in the English village. We began to wonder: if spaces in-between buildings could be understood to be at least as important as buildings themselves, could non-clinical spaces in-between clinical spaces assert as much priority in healthcare design as the clinical spaces themselves?

Most of the available literature on healthcare design at the time was related to minimal space standards and service delivery, rather than a more holistic model focused on the comforts of home and the dignity of choice. We were surprised and delighted, however, to find examples of bright, spacious, commodious settings for healthcare

Cultiv
the
'In-Bet
Humanisi
Modern
Experi

Corridors and waiting rooms are as important to the patient experience as clinical spaces. Yet in modernist hospitals they tend to be isolating, soul-destroying places to be. Since the 1970s, Toronto-based Montgomery Sisam Architects have been redressing the balance, enhancing patient wellbeing

Terry Montgomery

ating

ween'

ng the

Healthcare

ence

and restoring a connection to the great outdoors by focusing on the porch, the gallery and the courtyard. **Terry Montgomery,** one of the firm's cofounders, here cites their inspirations, from traditional towns and centuries-old hospitals to modern urban theorists, and presents some of their recent buildings.

created well before the 20th century. Hôtel-Dieu de Beaune in France, founded in 1443, was established as a hospital for the poor. The patients' ward, the 'Room for the Poor' as it was referred to, was furnished with two rows of large, curtained beds positioned around a lofty, bright central space where meals were served. In the Royal Chelsea Hospital in London, designed by Christopher Wren in 1690, curtained beds were clustered around a fireplace and wood-panelled sitting room. In both cases the space in-between is not only significant and meaningful, but also privileged in the design. We began to wonder whether the miracle of modern medical science had eliminated the healing and therapeutic qualities of the traditional care environment.

It was a fortuitous coincidence for Montgomery Sisam that, in the late 1970s, our first commissions in the healthcare sector were long-term care facilities for frail and vulnerable seniors. At this time, Aldo van Eyck was raising awareness about the reciprocal relationships between separate realms – inside and outside, city and institution, public and private – asking: 'Man still breathes both in and out. When is Modern architecture going to do the same?'[3] Designing for people with limited ability to venture beyond their immediate surroundings presented us with an invaluable opportunity to answer Van Eyck's query, revive pre-modern concepts of healing, and test our ideas about building for comfort and wellbeing. With renewed attention to the spaces in-between, the firm challenged assumptions and investigated new approaches to healthcare planning that honoured specific site conditions, promoting sustainability and fostering renewal not only within the institution itself, but also in its surrounding context.

The Spaces In-Between: The Porch, the Courtyard and the Gallery

We focused our attention on three elements: the porch, the gallery and the garden court, which allowed us to reconnect once-isolated realms and introduce a new vitality to our design approach in healthcare. The porch is neither inside nor outside, but a mediating place between two worlds: the busy, unpredictable public realm of the street and the structured, private realm of the institution. It both enhances the street and introduces the character and materiality of the interior while providing a protected place for people arriving at or departing from the main entrance. Here, one can experience the freedom and movement of the public realm with the shelter and security of the interior. Alternatively, the courtyard introduces natural light, seasonal variation and vegetation to the building interior, and can be a refreshing antidote to the monotonous uniformity of clinical space. The gallery complements the courtyard, ensuring a close, continuous yet controlled connection with the exterior while circulating between departments. Single-loaded with sliding doors, the gallery is a mutable space that can transform with the seasons; it is sometimes part of the interior and sometimes part of the exterior. Both individually and collectively, these elements allow the outdoors to be an integral part of the building programme and privilege the health and healing this promotes.

Whether in a hospital, mental health facility or long-term care home, reinvigorating these spaces in-between allows Montgomery Sisam to shift focus from the clinical to the non-clinical and breathe new life into the care environment, as is evidenced in the following three of the practice's projects.

Therapy in a Grove of White Pines

The Southdown Institute, completed in 2014, is a mental health and addictions treatment centre for the vowed religious located in a rural suburb of Newmarket, Ontario. It includes accommodation for 22 clients, treatment spaces and offices for clinicians, a food service and dining room as well as recreational facilities and a chapel. The spaces in-between – a large courtyard, small lobby, and L-shaped gallery – define the parti and serve to advance the health-promoting qualities of the building's natural surroundings.

A modest canopy greets clients as they arrive, introducing the intimate scale of the building. The courtyard is the primary organising element, situated in the centre of the plan. Embracing a stand of tall white pines, it is not only a focal point, but also a place of respite, reflection and renewal. In the summer months, sliding doors open directly onto a terrace in the courtyard, making it an integral part of the life and activity of the building. In the winter months, the ever-changing quality of light seen through the trees penetrates the gallery. The primary circulation component, the gallery, bounds the courtyard, linking all major public spaces and doubling as a breakout space for group sessions. Numerous other spaces in the building meet all of the requirements of the functional programme, but it is these spaces in-between that establish a sense of place, promote the restorative merits of the natural setting and offer greater meaning to the institution.

Montgomery Sisam Architects

Southdown Institute

Newmarket

Ontario

2014

top: Situated in a tranquil, wooded setting, the beauty of the natural surroundings of this treatment care centre is an integral part of the healing environment for the clergy and the vowed religious. The plan wraps carefully around a stand of mature white pines to create a courtyard, the focal point of a community dedicated to the growth and healing of its members.

right: The new facility is exceptionally progressive in promoting a positive stimulating environment. The courtyard and terrace become an integral part of the building during summer months, offering opportunities for social engagement and/or quiet contemplation.

opposite: The entrance lobby affords direct access to the gallery and the courtyard just beyond, providing an immediate sense of sanctuary and inviting members to explore the surrounding landscape.

1. LOBBY
2. CHAPEL
3. OFFICES
4. COURTYARD DECK
5. STAFF DINING ROOM
6. RESIDENT DINING ROOM
7. KITCHEN
8. THE GREAT ROOM
9. MULTI-PURPOSE ROOM
10. GROUP THERAPY ROOMS
11. MEDITATION ROOM
12. FITNESS ROOM
13. ART STUDIO

It is these spaces in-between that establish a sense of place, promote the restorative merits of the natural setting and offer greater meaning to the institution.

Embracing a Treasured Park

St John's Rehab at Sunnybrook Health
Sciences is an addition to an existing
hospital in suburban Toronto. Designed by
Montgomery Sisam Architects with Farrow
Partnership, it was completed in 2010.
The addition includes a new, accessible
entrance to the hospital complex, two large
rehabilitation gyms, additional clinical offices
and a therapeutic swimming pool. The primary
in-between spaces consist of a large entrance
canopy and vestibule, a double-height roof
monitor and lobby, a feature stairway and a
two-level, single-loaded gallery around a large
therapeutic garden.

The plan is anchored around the double-
height roof monitor marking the main
entrance and lobby. Upon arrival under the
canopy, there are views directly across the
lobby space into the therapeutic garden and
park beyond. The feature stairway provides
tangible acknowledgement of the change in
grade between entry level and garden level.
The L-shaped gallery provides a link at two
levels to the existing building to the west, and
access to two new therapeutic gyms to the
south. It also affords informal therapy space
for patients before and after treatment. While
the generic 'big-box' block for the therapy
gyms and offices can be easily adapted to
different clinical programmes, the glazed
gallery and relationships that are established
between entrance, garden and stairway are
designed to endure.

The addition is designed to refocus the
hospital community around an existing
treed lawn and garden. The park-like setting,
nurtured and maintained by the Sisters of St
John the Divine since the relocation of the
hospital to its present site in 1930, had been
violated and diminished in recent years, first
with the construction of a five-storey inpatient
tower, and then with ongoing pressure to
expand surface parking lots. This green space,
now revitalised and interwoven with the life
of the hospital, provides an enduring and
sustainable natural resource within the city.

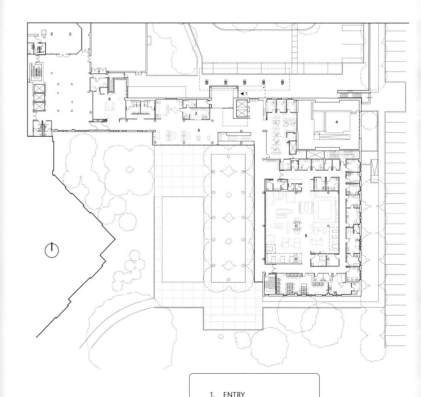

1. ENTRY
2. RECEPTION
3. LOBBY
4. THERAPY POOL
5. TREATMENT GYM
6. GIFT SHOP

Montgomery Sisam Architects with
Farrow Partnership Architects

St John's Rehab

Sunnybrook Health Sciences

Toronto

2010

left: A generous, single-loaded gallery provides primary circulation for the addition at both levels and provides access to many new treatment spaces. It also offers views of the courtyard, therapy garden, landscaped areas beyond, and hydrotherapy pool below.

bottom: A large, accessible porch offers shelter to clients as they arrive and depart. Clear sight lines from the porch through to the gallery and park beyond establish a coherent framework for intuitive wayfinding.

opposite top: The courtyard provides a focal point for the new addition, which also re-establishes the connection between the hospital and its treed parkland. It revives the holistic idea of health as was first intended when locating the hospital in such a unique natural setting.

opposite bottom: The entry porch, L-shaped gallery and garden courtyard frame the simple shoebox plan of this addition to a suburban rehabilitation hospital. The various clinical functions are arranged so as to be readily adapted to suit future modifications, whereas the gallery and its relationship to the garden are designed to endure.

This green space, now revitalised and interwoven with the life of the hospital, provides an enduring and sustainable natural resource within the city.

A House in a Garden in the City

Ronald McDonald House in Toronto, completed in 2011, is located in a downtown residential neighbourhood that is adjacent to one of the city's pre-eminent hospital precincts. The building provides accommodation for 81 out-of-town families with seriously ill children receiving medical treatment at the nearby Hospital for Sick Children (also known as SickKids – see p 20). It strives to enhance its residents' quality of life as a place of calm, comfort and respite – a refuge from the clinical setting while still supporting a myriad of special needs and physical limitations. In addition to the family suites, facilities include a living room, dining area, kitchen, library, fitness room, administrative offices and support spaces.

The building, located on a T-shaped site in an urban neighbourhood, is configured around three landscaped courtyards: a walled garden forecourt with water fountain, an active play and dining area, and a quiet retreat with a spare green lawn and walkway. Glazed galleries bound each courtyard, providing circulation, compelling views and natural light throughout the four-storey house. These elements are the essence of spaces in-between; they achieve ready access to natural light, air and animated street views through multiple indoor and outdoor connections – a counterpoint to the traditional clinical environment. In so doing, these spaces maintain a sense of normalcy within the residence, offering a care environment where kids can be kids to the fullest extent possible.

Montgomery Sisam Architects

Ronald McDonald House

Toronto

2011

above: The gallery overlooks each of the communal courts and out onto the city, offering residents positive stimulation with ample natural light, through-ventilation and animated views.

right: The plan for this urban home-away-from-home for sick children and their families exploits a shallow floor-plate to address the street frontages and create a series of landscaped garden courts. Each court has a distinct function: to greet families, inspire children's play and provide for quiet contemplation.

opposite: The covered porch and walled court afford children and their families a transition between the public realm of the street and the private refuge of the residence.

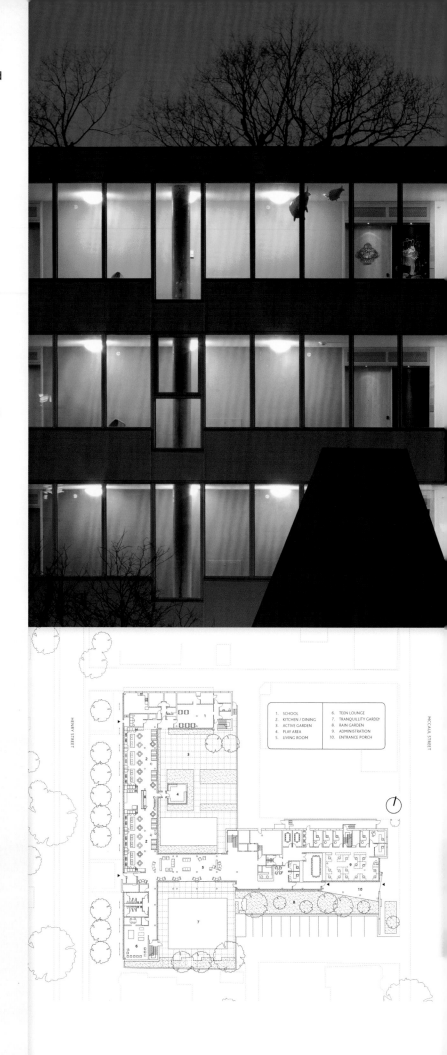

1. SCHOOL
2. KITCHEN / DINING
3. ACTIVE GARDEN
4. PLAY AREA
5. LIVING ROOM
6. TEEN LOUNGE
7. TRANQUILLITY GARDEN
8. RAIN GARDEN
9. ADMINISTRATION
10. ENTRANCE PORCH

HENRY STREET

MCCAUL STREET

A Holistic Approach to Healthcare Planning

Spaces in-between, so essential in pre-modern care environments, have come to define Montgomery Sisam's attitude to designing for health and wellbeing. These non-clinical spaces, such as the porch, courtyard and gallery, offer invaluable opportunities for us, as architects, to humanise our expanding healthcare infrastructure and enrich the care experience. Serving now as anchors in our approach to planning, they mediate between the highly technical, ever-changing clinical world of the contemporary healthcare institution and the more holistic, integrated world of the traditional care setting. Spaces in-between allow us to connect the unique attributes of the site with the specific requirements of the programme. With renewed emphasis on that which resonates so acutely with the wellbeing of occupants – the meaningful, enduring qualities of the outdoors – we can establish sustainable, forward-thinking frameworks for institutions that enrich not only the care environment but also the larger public realm.[4] ◮

Notes
1. Jane Jacobs, *The Death and Life of Great American Cities*, Random House (New York), 1961.
2. Gordon Cullen, *The Concise Townscape*, Architectural Press (New York), 1961.
3. Aldo van Eyck, 'Kaleidoscope of the Mind', *VIA 1: Ecology of the Mind*, Graduate School of Fine Arts, University of Pennsylvania (Philadelphia, PA), 1968, p 90.
4. For further reading, see Montgomery Sisam Architects, *Place and Occasion*, Artifice-Books on Architecture (London), 2013.

Sunand Prasad

Penoyre & Prasad,
New QEII Hospital,
Welwyn Garden City,
Hertfordshire,
UK,
2015

The courtyard is an active part
of the design of the building,
bringing greenery and light to
the entrance hall and providing
a calm view from all the waiting
spaces, as well as organising
the floor plans.

Regenerative Agents Patient-Focused Architectures

Holistic care is nothing new. There are well-known examples across the world and throughout history – from ancient Greece, China and India to early 20th-century northern Europe – of approaches that prioritise placemaking as a facilitator for health and healing. Inspired by such precedents, London-based architects Penoyre & Prasad produce buildings that engage with nature and help put patients back in control of their recovery process. **Sunand Prasad**, one of the firm's cofounders, explains.

When Penoyre & Prasad was founded in 1988, the idea of 'patient-focused medicine' was beginning to gain currency. The phrase was a powerful three-word critique of what had prevailed unchallenged for some decades: that doctor knows best and that a disease-free future was around the corner thanks to modern scientific methods and technological advances. In an extraordinarily trenchant article in *The Lancet* in 1974, Ivan Illich had written:

> By transforming pain, illness, and death from a personal challenge into a technical problem, medical practice expropriates the potential of people to deal with their human condition in an autonomous way and becomes the source of a new kind of un-health.[1]

It seemed evident, then, that in trying to pursue science-based design to serve science-based medicine, healthcare designers had abandoned the conscious creation of place as a primary task of architecture in favour of the accommodation of medical processes. So much so that the hospital corridor had become the epitome of alienating, bewildering placelessness. Philip Larkin's poem 'The Building', also from 1974 and prompted by his visit to Kingston General Hospital in London, sums it up perfectly:

> For past these doors are rooms, and rooms past those,
> And more rooms yet, each one further off
>
> And harder to return from …[2]

Penoyre & Prasad's designs for healthcare have thus been animated by a search within architecture and urbanism for the equivalent of patient-focused medicine.

The Environment as Healer

Until the advent of modern medicine, and particularly the development of antibiotics in the 20th century, which appeared to have eliminated the threat of infectious diseases, the environment had been a central part of curing illness and restoring health in cultures around the world. In ancient Greece the sick went to be healed at the shrines of Asclepius, the god of medicine. In China and India, systems of geometric ordering of buildings, Feng Shui and the Vastu Shastras, were related closely to the balance of bodily humours. Etymologically, the word 'hospital' derives from the latin *hospes*, or guest, so it was originally a place for caring for guests, and not necessarily the sick. Filippo Brunelleschi's seminal Ospedale degli Innocenti (1419–45), a foundlings' hospital in Florence, was a place of asylum and shelter. When hospitals in the modern sense started to be built in Europe in the 18th century, their architects set considerable store by plan configurations and sectional proportions, particularly of inpatient wards. No one was more explicit than Florence Nightingale in linking the design of wards to patients' recovery. In her *Notes on Nursing* of 1859, she wrote:

> they [patients] should be able, without raising themselves or turning in bed, to see out of window from their beds, to see sky and sun-light at least, if you can show them nothing else, I assert to be, if not of the very first importance for recovery, at least something very near it.[3]

Similar convictions informed early Modernist medical architecture, such as Johannes Duicker's Zonnestraal sanatorium in Hilversum, the Netherlands (1928) and Alvar Aalto's Paimio Sanatorium in Finland (1933 – see p 59).

The Evolution of Therapeutic Environments

Two conceptions characterise these essays in the creation of therapeutic environments: the unity of mind and body on the one hand, and on the other the pre-eminence of nature as an agent of healing. The environment, through daylight, fresh air, scent, modulated sound, crisp linen, views of greenery and gardens, affects the body's physical mechanisms as well as the workings of the mind, including its perception simply of being cared for.

The remarkable achievements of scientifically based medicine had, by the middle of the 20th century, shifted the focus of healing entirely to the body as an assemblage of physical parts, and elevated the status of the physician to the all-knowing master of cures. The separation of body and mind in medicine was perhaps further cemented by the development of the treatment of mental illness as its own sophisticated quasi-scientific discipline.

The powerful medical methods, processes and techniques that now needed to be accommodated found a reflection in a new architectural paradigm: the concept of the hospital itself as a great scientific medical instrument. Hospital planning became increasingly deterministic, organised by body parts and clinical processes – an approach that still dominates the design of healthcare environments around the world, albeit with increasing acknowledgment of people's experience.

Best practice in medicine, however, now seeks to harness patients' own knowledge as part of the diagnostic task, and their own regenerative power in the restoration of health. It embraces systems thinking, taking into account the wider life circumstances of patients, and recognising that social and economic conditions are strongly linked to health and wellbeing. In this holistic vision there remains nevertheless a secure place for specialism, and for segmentation by body part, which has brought about great surgical and medical advances.

New QEII Hospital, Welwyn Garden City

The New QEII Hospital in Hertfordshire, opened in 2015, is the latest example of Penoyre & Prasad's search for a new typology truly reflective of patient-centred medicine and care. It enshrines three principles.

Firstly, the building's organisation and its spaces are designed as places for indeterminate interchange and flow as well as the specific requirements of clinical processes. The entrance, circulation and waiting spaces are a connected field of areas for informal meeting and, for example, the display of art – a world apart from the utilitarianism of hospital corridors. Secondly, these areas and the interiors generally are strongly connected with exterior space, to nature and to the public realm, to the point of dissolving the boundary between them. Both of these design strategies are further supported by the making of a strong urban form for what is a civic building of great social purpose. Thirdly, in the selection of materials and details of construction are embodied regenerative, zero-waste principles inspired by natural systems.

above: The interior circulation spaces of the New QEII Hospital are designed to provide a great deal of transparency and diagonal views rendering the whole building as legible as possible. Specially commissioned artwork and complementary signage design add a layer of richness as well as utility.

left: Two of the flanks of the three-sided plan, facing the public realm and entrance route, have colonnades leading to the main entrance, the urgent care entrance and community spaces. The roof profile, with its asymmetric pitches, acknowledges the Garden City context.

The New QEII is among the first of a new generation of National Health Service (NHS) hospitals integrating primary, sub-acute and social care services to serve the local population, who were also involved in the brief and design. The extensive range of services provided includes urgent care, diagnostic imaging, large outpatients and therapies departments, ambulatory care and an endoscopy suite. The clinical layouts, with their many generic spaces, enable flexibility of use, day to day, and adaptability to future service changes. Inpatient beds, the surgical unit, intensive care and the emergency department are provided in the nearby Lister Hospital.

The building is formed of three L-shaped wings enfolding a central courtyard, around which the main public circulation and all of the waiting spaces are arranged. The geometry also creates smaller, more private gardens at the edge against an old mature hedgerow, ensuring that people in the building are never far from the calming presence of gardens. A generous, timber-lined colonnade connects arrival routes from opposite directions and leads to the main entrance with its central reception, cafe, pharmacy, and information and community support facilities. The bright and open triple-height main entrance space connects the internal space, colonnade and landscaped courtyard, views to which are immediately visible on entry.

The pitches of the long roofs and the glazed porcelain tiles on the walls acknowledge the Arts and Crafts roots of Welwyn Garden City. These tiled facades are lifted up above the colonnade to spatially link the urban public realm to the courtyard within. The windows generally incorporate a large fixed-glass pane and an insulated shutter, which form part of the natural ventilation.

Energy requirements have been minimised through the building form and fabric. Air source heat pumps, heat recovery ventilation and high-efficiency lighting fulfil the residual demand. The building's carbon emissions have been reduced further through the use of renewable energy generation. Climate adaptation was also fully considered in the design through its inclusion in the pioneering UK government-funded Design for A Future Climate research project.

Penoyre & Prasad,
Guy's Tower External Retrofit,
Guy's Hospital, London, 2014

above: Guy's Tower, with its new high-performance skin. The 'communication tower' on the right is clad with specially folded dark-grey anodised aluminium, the facets of which reflect the changing weather. The flat pale umber strip runs up the tower in front of the boiler flues and terminates in a light sculpture designed to be programmed to react to fuel use. The 'user tower' on the left is re-clad with curtain walling outside the existing external wall, installed from balconies using special access systems without any disruption to occupants.

Computer thermal modelling was used to rapidly test alternative external cladding strategies from a complete double skin to a minimal upgrade of the windows. The design at the far right was finally selected for maximum performance within the budget: a new highly insulated skin outside the existing envelope that was removed gradually from inside to make more space.

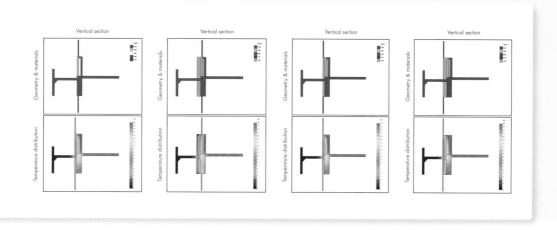

Penoyre & Prasad,
Sir Ludwig Guttmann Health & Wellbeing Centre,
East Village,
London,
2011

left: The health and community centre is organised around a four-storey atrium, the west wall of which adjoins a courtyard. The atrium is an extension of the urban public realm and has multiple uses.

above: Despite its relatively small size in comparison to the large residential block of East Village, originally designed and constructed as the Athletes' Village for the London 2012 Olympic Games, the building's profile gives it a distinct monumental presence expressive of its civic role.

Guy's Tower External Retrofit, London

Not every project will have scope to embrace all three principles outlined above. At the 34-storey Guy's Tower, constructed in 1974, the tallest hospital building in the world, the brief was limited to making the crumbling and tired-looking exterior 'fit for purpose' for the next 30 years and reflective of a modern, high-performing hospital and health service; and to do so without any disruption to the services.

Neither the interior planning nor the mechanical, electrical and plumbing services were part of the project, but working with engineers and project managers from Arup, Penoyre & Prasad expanded 'fitness for purpose' to include the energy and carbon as well as the aesthetic challenge, while also using the opportunity to transform the rather mean circulation spaces into the connective field described above. In the event, the world financial crisis of 2008 to 2010 forced a scaling back of the project, and the improvements to the internal circulation were abandoned. Externally, the original concrete walls were made safe and then entirely over-clad with aluminium and curtain walling over a highly insulated substratum, all installed working entirely from outside, using existing balconies and clever access systems devised by the contractor Balfour Beatty. Detailed computational thermal modelling was used to refine the environmental design and predict energy use.

The tower, a familiar part of the London skyline, though described as Brutalist owes as much to Constructivism, being an expressive composition in two parts. The stack of floor plates of the 'user tower', each surrounded by a continuous balcony, are connected by the second, 'communication tower' with its dramatic overhang of a lecture theatre on the 31st floor. The new design emphasised the verticality of the communication tower, cladding it in dark aluminium panels with a stiffening origami fold for the outer skin, juxtaposed with a flat pale-umber strip running up to the boiler flue terminations and crowned by a sculpture by German artist Carsten Nicolai. Cleaning the balcony fronts of the user tower has strengthened the horizontals of the floors. The re-cladding has not sought to transform the somewhat gawky architecture of the original, but sharpened its contours and added sparkle to the skin, the facets of which reflect the changing London sky.

Sir Ludwig Guttmann Health & Wellbeing Centre, London

In the last two decades, the UK has been making a decisive shift to a primary and community care led National Health Service, ending the dominance of the acute sector. A stimulating challenge for architects has been the design of a new typology, neither GP surgery nor hospital, to create civic buildings of substantial scale, the mission of which is as much the promotion of health and wellbeing as the treatment of disease. The Northern Ireland Health Service has led the way in implementing this approach, and Penoyre & Prasad has so far designed six such buildings in Belfast, with locally based Todd Architects.

As these were being designed in the early 2000s, the NHS Local Improvement Finance Trust (LIFT) programme in England triggered similar innovations with new types of community and integrated care centres. At the centre of these is the idea of the service being configured around the patient, rather than the patient having to navigate a disaggregated, provider-centred service. In southeast Belfast, over 40 separate buildings have been replaced by three strategically located integrated health and social care centres, and a similar 'one-stop shop' approach has been pursued elsewhere in the UK.

Penoyre & Prasad's design for the Sir Ludwig Guttmann Health & Wellbeing Centre in East Village, London, which opened in 2011, builds on the typology developed initially for integrated care centres in Belfast. The many cellular spaces required for consultation, diagnosis, treatment and surgical procedures are gathered on four floors around a forum created by extending the urban public realm into the building. On entering this lofty, generously day-lit atrium from the street, visitors pass by a pharmacy and a cafe, spaces that have more in common with retail than with healthcare. They can also walk straight through the space and out into a secluded garden courtyard, ameliorating any sense of being trapped in an institution.

Unlike the clinical spaces to which it may lead, the atrium is functionally indeterminate. As well as making the building easy to navigate, it provides circulation, is used for waiting, and could even hold a large meeting, exhibition or other event. There is a fitness suite and spaces for community use on the first floor.

The centre was built to high environmental standards, using natural ventilation, and renewable energy with careful selection of materials and the recycling of over 90 per cent of already minimised construction waste. Originally the medical centre for the London 2012 Olympic Games, it occupies a tight triangular site edged by railway cuttings at a prominent entry point into the Olympic Park. Its integration into the urban fabric, its history, and its role as one of only two civic buildings in East Village is reflected in its sculptural form. Compared to the residential blocks it sits among, the centre is relatively small. Inspired by the monumental presence of the diminutive Trinity Church among Manhattan's skyscrapers, the design gives it a profile and compositional presence that emphasise its specialness. The pavement is extended into a colonnade containing all the main and subsidiary entrances, further integrating the building into its urban setting.

Regenerative Agents

The mastery of efficient clinical planning and logistics is essential to the success of any healthcare design, but by itself insufficient. In Penoyre & Prasad's projects it is seen simply as a precondition for the pursuit of the experiential, expressive, social and ecological ambitions of the architecture. Feedback from earlier buildings by the practice has shown that the design principles described above, together with an organisational culture of focusing on patients' needs at the centre, achieve the immediate aim of giving patients a sense of control and help to minimise the stresses inevitable when dealing with medical conditions. Within their landscapes and urban settings, the larger ambition is to make the buildings themselves agents in the therapeutic scheme, and beyond that, agents of wellbeing. ⌂

Notes
1. Ivan Illich, 'Medical Nemesis', *The Lancet*, 11 May 1974, pp 918–21. Republished at http://jech.bmj.com/content/57/12/919.full.
2. See Philip Larkin, *High Windows*, Faber & Faber (London), 2003, pp 136–8.
3. Florence Nightingale, *Notes on Nursing*, facsimile edition, JB Lippincott Company (Philadelphia, PA), 1946, p 48. Digital version available at: https://babel.hathitrust.org/cgi/pt?id=uc2.ark:/13960/t1xd16d8p;view=1up;seq=9.

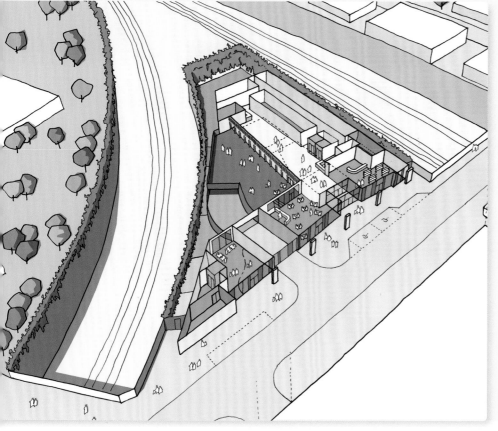

The ground-floor layout connects the building to its urban and social context, where its healthcare purpose, though large in terms of floor area, is but one of a number of uses and destinations.

Transforming Hospitals

Building Restorative Healthcare

COUNTERPOINT 02/2017 No 246

Robin Guenther

Our planet is sick; so what hope for us who live on it? **Robin Guenther**, principal of international design practice Perkins+Will and Senior Advisor to the non-profit coalition Health Care Without Harm, argues that architecture for health is about more than curing human illness. It is also about regenerative design, where buildings become net resource generators rather than resource consumers, and where initiatives are established to prevent the causes of epidemics such as obesity, asthma and diabetes. The ongoing existence of healthy, thriving communities depends on it.

The theme of this issue, therapeutic approaches to sustainable architecture, reveals that the design of healthcare spaces has indeed entered an era of radical transformation. Two pivotal questions emerge from this exploration: Are we using health as our inspiration to transform the design of healthcare settings? Are we witnessing the emergence of 21st-century restorative healthcare architecture? I believe the answer to both is yes, but we must move more aggressively and assertively beyond sustainable design to truly embrace the tenets of restorative and regenerative design thinking.

Hospitals have always reflected both the healthcare systems that produce them, and societal perceptions of disease. The 20th-century hospital, in its quest to accommodate rapid and chaotic changes in urbanisation and suburbanisation, medical care delivery, and medical and construction technologies, relegated a vision of 'healing', 'wholeness' and connection to nature to the past. As Annmarie Adams remarks in her article: 'ours is not the golden age of hospitals' (p 18). But the projects profiled in this issue suggest a new convergence of humanism and sustainability in healing spaces that is fundamentally changing the typology of healthcare.

Can traditional healthcare organisations be leveraged to catalyse transformation within their own walls and in their communities to bend the chronic disease curve, fundamentally reducing the environmental, social and economic causations of asthma, obesity and diabetes? Central to these questions is the axiom, 'First, do no harm'. This seminal principle embraces a broad definition of health and recognises that prevention and restoration are preferable to treatment on a planet with a finite carrying capacity.

For designers and architects, this requires a new focus on prioritising health, and finding built-environment solutions that solve far more than one problem, and do not create new ones: built-environment solutions that 'do no harm' and in fact 'heal' some of the harm we have already done – a perfect metaphor for the healthcare sector. Globally, the green building movement is moving beyond conceiving of buildings as resource consumers towards 'regenerative design' thinking, where buildings are designed with the inherent capability to become net resource generators rather than resource consumers. Regenerative design offers a global vision for a resilient and restorative health delivery system that contributes to a stronger, fairer and cleaner world economy based on one simple truth: we will not have healthy people on a sick planet.

Perkins+Will, Spaulding Rehabilitation Hospital, Boston, Massachusetts, 2014

A unique confluence of programme and place, the building restored a contaminated parcel of land as a metaphor for restoring rehabilitation patients to health. It features operable windows and a range of outdoor spaces to connect patients to the sound of birds and boats on Boston Harbor.

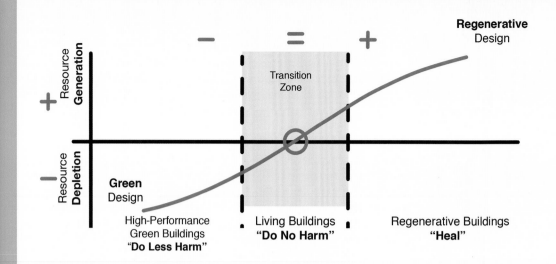

Robin Guenther,
Regenerative design
diagram,
2013

Sustainable practices 'do
no harm', while restorative
practices 'heal' some of
the harm that has already
been done. Regenerative
design creates a cascading
series of benefits instead of
externalised harm.

The healthcare industry is in a pivotal position to lead a reintegration of social, economic, environmental, health and resource-balanced sustainable practices in service of restoration and healing. The sector can move beyond a focus on doing 'less harm' to a future that positively contributes to the conditions that foster individual, community and global health.

What is Health in the 21st Century?

What is health? The authors of this issue generally concur with the World Health Organization definition, which suggests that health is a state of physical, mental and social wellbeing, and not merely the absence of disease or infirmity.[1] The farmer and essayist Wendell Berry has said that health is membership.[2] The word 'health', he claims, comes from the same Indo-European root as 'heal', 'whole' and 'holy'. To be healthy is literally to be whole. To heal is to make whole.

Any contemporary discussion of health cannot underestimate the looming impacts of climate change on planetary health and the future of healthcare delivery. In 2015, the UK Lancet Commission on Health and Climate Change proclaimed: 'climate change represents an unacceptably high and potentially catastrophic risk to human health.'[3] The report further suggests that impacts from climate change have the potential to undo more than 50 years of global public health gains. What is health in a world with increasing water scarcity and food insecurity? What is health in a world with rising sea levels, submerged islands, and increasing extreme weather events? We can, and must, accelerate the rate of adaptation of our built environments to meet the shifting realities of the 21st century.

Can the healthcare industry become a model for the larger world in developing a 'holistic' ecological approach to these environmental and health challenges? It is time to redefine the role of healthcare institutions as pivotal agents for creating and supporting the conditions for healthy and thriving communities that support individual health and wellbeing. The healthcare sector can and should be a

Perkins+Will
and Mazzetti,
Kaiser Permanente
Small Hospital,
Big Idea
competition,
New York,
2014

In this winning entry, the
public space of the hospital
is re-imagined as a place of
health promotion, including
a 'thrive bar' for help with
mobile health devices, health
demonstrations, an exercise
area, restaurant, community
garden and cookery school.

catalyst for defining and promoting health for the benefit of communities, but today its influence is largely confined to specific disease-management activities at an individual level.

Until now, we have accepted that our built environments are accompanied by a set of negative unintended consequences: sedentary lifestyles, greenhouse gas emissions, chemical exposures – consequences that are displaced in both space and time. We did not intend car-dependent development patterns to cause obesity and diabetes, yet they contribute to the epidemic. We did not intend fossil fuel use in buildings to cause climate change, yet it does. We believe these unintended consequences are the inevitable price of 'progress' – but we need to find another way.

Many of the authors in this issue explore how salutogenesis – the exploration of the causes of health – can help us find a path forward in the design of restorative hospital buildings. Perkins+Will's winning competition entry for a net-zero energy small hospital for the Kaiser Permanente integrated managed care consortium examined how the public realm of hospitals might be reimagined as 'regenerative places of health', a theme explored in depth in the work of Montgomery Sisam in this issue. Arup defines the 21st-century imperative for low-energy and net-zero resource hospitals (pp 48–55). In the US, Mahlum's Peace Island Medical Center (2012), located on an island near Seattle, is the first attempt to create a net-zero energy and water use hospital. While it did not succeed in meeting the rigorous requirements of the Living Building Challenge, it has demonstrated that such achievement is possible.

What is healthcare for, if not to serve as the vision-keeper of community health and wellness? Guest-Editor Terri Peters has brilliantly outlined the problem of healthcare spaces as well as innovative solutions to reducing energy use and toxic materials in her Introduction to this issue. Michael Murphy and Jerry Mansfield of MASS Design Group demonstrate in their GHESKIO Cholera Treatment Center, Haiti (2015) (pp 88–9) that a healthcare delivery facility can be combined with wastewater treatment facilities in order to mitigate continued contamination of water that transmits the disease. This solution demonstrates restorative and regenerative principles in action. Murphy and Mansfield argue that 'form follows facts', and that we are entering an era where owners will demand evidence and measurement of architecture's impact on health – 'to prove it is worth the investment'.

Resilience

At the same time, the healthcare industry is just beginning to articulate the impact of climate change on services delivery. As average temperatures rise, heat island impacts in dense urban areas will exacerbate chronic respiratory conditions in the elderly and children. More extreme weather events – hurricanes and tsunamis in coastal areas, tornadoes and floods, fires and drought – will require a more resilient emergency-care infrastructure capable of delivering essential community services, such as reliable power and potable water, as well as healthcare.

Perkins+Will,
Spaulding
Rehabilitation
Hospital,
Boston,
Massachusetts,
2014

This is the first Boston waterfront building designed to withstand 50-year projections for sea-level rise and storm surge. All infrastructure is located on the roof; the building is energy efficient and generates electricity through on-site combined heat and power.

As we move towards restorative and regenerative built solutions, our buildings become inherently more resilient, as evident in Perkins+Will's Spaulding Rehabilitation Hospital (2014) in Boston, Massachusetts. Buildings powered by on-site renewable energy, for example, can continue to function when power grids are disrupted. Buildings that rely on daylighting can operate without electrical lighting for much of the day. Stephen Verderber's article (pp 100–107) is a valuable contribution to the understanding that preservation of a community's social networks during and after adverse events is imperative, and that portable structures that provide uninterrupted care aid 'in fostering reaffirmative, place-reattachment behaviours, behaviours prerequisite to effective community rebuilding'. He laments the difficulty of placing portable structures within the broader discursive streams in architecture, finding that healthcare architects lack an 'attitude of public service, outreach, empathy and compassion' for the broader aspects of community cohesion beyond the four walls.

Healthcare as the New Civic Architecture

Together, these individual efforts form a persuasive argument that it is time for healthcare to shift attention from the causes of diseases to the upstream causes of health, in place-based, resilient, community-led promotion, prevention and management programmes. Julian Weyer notes CF Møller's focus on 'reconnecting the often-isolated healthcare complexes to the city and society' (pp 32–41). There are new forms of community health centres, integrating health services with libraries, community centres and community gardens. Imagine if these buildings were powered by renewable resources and acted as community safe havens in extreme weather, as in Farrow Partnership's 2013 winning competition entry for Protea Health in South Africa? The team's bold vision underscores its design approach: 'A new world must shift attention beyond the causes of diseases to the causes of health.'[4]

Addressing health vulnerability at an urban scale has not generally been considered the purview of health systems, but the impacts of large health campuses on health outcomes of surrounding communities are the focus of emerging 'health district' design explorations by a number of leading US firms. In recent planning work completed for the Baton Rouge Health District, Perkins+Will identified a diverse set of projects and programmes that address emergency preparedness as well as everyday health. These included implementation of a complete street network, creation of a street-level Obesity and Diabetes Center, and implementation of an open-space network that supports sustainable stormwater management while enhancing access to nature and spaces for active bicycle and walking commutes.

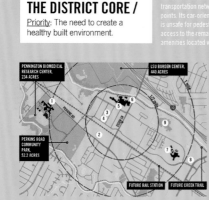

THE DISTRICT CORE /

Priority: The need to create a healthy built environment.

The District core has an insufficient transportation network with few access points. Its car-oriented built environment is unsafe for pedestrians. There is limited access to the remarkable green space amenities located within walking distance.

PENNINGTON BIOMEDICAL RESEARCH CENTER, 234 ACRES

LSU BURDEN CENTER, 440 ACRES

PERKINS ROAD COMMUNITY PARK, 52.2 ACRES

FUTURE RAIL STATION   FUTURE CREEK TRAIL

PRELIMINARY INDICATORS

INTERSECTION DENSITY (WALKABILITY)

9 INTERSECTIONS
are located within a 1/4 mile in the district core.

25-30 INTERSECTIONS
are typically located within a 1/4 mile in a walkable environment that supports transit use.

ACRES OF PARK LAND

6.4 ACRES
of park land are available per 1,000 residents in Baton Rouge.

13.8 ACRES
is the median amount of park land per 1,000 residents in similar metropolitan areas.

HOW WE'LL MEASURE PROGRESS

INTERSECTION DENSITY
SIDEWALK COVERAGE
PEDESTRIAN / BIKE ACCIDENTS
ACRES OF PUBLIC OPEN SPACE
% OF FAST FOOD RESTAURANTS
% TRANSIT COVERAGE
PARKING DEMAND
DIVERSITY OF LAND USES
DIVERSITY OF BUSINESS TYPES
HOUSING UNITS

The Path Forward

The architecture of hospitals appears to be on the threshold of simultaneously building bridges to both the 18th and 21st centuries, inspired by evidence-based design, therapeutic and sustainable design, and humanism, assisted by wireless technology and the miniaturisation of medical equipment. Increased understanding of the role of nature in healing, and the emphasis on the civic value of hospital buildings is, in a sense, a return to 18th-century values. Emerging 21st-century research on the relationship between the built environment and health across all scales – from the microscopic composition of increasingly toxic building materials to the health benefits of walkable, transit-oriented, nature-infused neighbourhoods – is influencing both healthcare settings and the broader practice of architecture. Finally, the convergence of traditional silos such as medicine and public health with architecture and urban design is broadening our social lenses. Our task is to translate this health focus to the design of our healing spaces in order to create truly restorative built environments. ᗺ

Perkins+Will, Baton Rouge Health District, Baton Rouge, Louisiana, 2016

left: This health district report demonstrates that large healthcare campuses often lack walkability, open space, and variety of uses that foster social cohesion and healthy behaviours.

Farrow Partnership, Ngonyama Okpanum & Associates and Clark Nexsen, Protea Health Promoting Lifestyle Center, South Africa (2013)

bottom: This inspiring winning competition entry uses the national flower of South Africa – the Protea – as the symbolic metaphor for healing and renewal, and for a safe and healthy gathering place. The Protea also inspired the prototypical and iconic building form, with the roof designed to mimic its petals.

Notes
1. World Health Organization: www. who.int/about/definition/en/print.html.
2. Wendell Berry, 'Health is Membership', in Norman Wirzba (ed), *The Art of the Commonplace: The Agrarian Essays of Wendell Berry*, Counterpoint (Washington DC), 2002.
3. Lancet Commission on Health and Climate Change, 'Health and Climate Change: Policy Responses to Protect Public Health', *The Lancet*, 23 June 2015: www.thelancet.com/ commissions/climate-change#Jun23.
4. www.designandhealth.com/farrow-okpanum-clark-nexsen.

CONTRIBUTORS

ARCHITECTURAL DESIGN

DESIGN FOR HEALTH

Annmarie Adams is jointly appointed in the School of Architecture and Department of Social Studies of Medicine at McGill University in Montreal. She is the author of *Medicine by Design: The Architect and the Modern Hospital, 1893–1943* (University of Minnesota Press, 2008). Her research on the intersections of medicine and architecture has garnered numerous awards, including the Christophe Pierre Award for Research Excellence, the Jason Hannah Medal from the Royal Society of Canada, a CIHR Health Career Award, and a YWCA Woman of Distinction prize. In 2015, she was elected to the College of Fellows of the Royal Architectural Institute of Canada.

Ann Marie Aguilar is an associate director at Arup Associates. She was the first WELL Accredited Professional (AP) outside the US and is a passionate advocate of regenerative sustainability and the impact of space design on human behaviour and performance. Her 17 years of global project experience range in scale from individual buildings to small city developments. She has extensive experience in LEED/WELL certifications, material deconstruction and material reuse processes. Her current focus is on bringing health and wellbeing strategies into the forefront of integrated design so that they are delivered as a seamless overarching framework.

Sean Ahlquist is an assistant professor of architecture at the Taubman College of Architecture and Urban Planning, University of Michigan. He holds a Master of Architecture from the Emergent Design and Technologies programme at the Architectural Association (AA) in London, and is completing his doctoral research at the Institute for Computational Design (ICD), University of Stuttgart. As a part of the interdisciplinary Cluster in Computational Media and Interactive Systems at the University of Michigan, his work connects architecture with material science, computer science, performing arts, interaction design and medicine.

Giuseppe Boscherini is an architect, industrial and interior designer with extensive experience leading and inspiring design teams within internationally renowned practices such as Foster + Partners, Gensler, IBI Group and Woods Bagot on multidisciplinary projects for global clients, including the NHS. Most recently, he was Creative Director at CBRE, facilitating client workshops, enhancing project content and leading research initiatives. He currently runs his own London-based co-creation studio, aiding clients' understanding, broadening their vision and assisting with their decision-making through the use of drawings, diagrams and vignettes. He previously taught professional practice to mature students at the KLC School of Design in London.

Costanza Colombi is a research assistant professor in the Department of Psychiatry at the University of Michigan. Her research interests include early signs, developmental trajectories, and intervention in Autism Spectrum Disorder (ASD), with an emphasis on the efficacy and effectiveness of intervention for children with ASD. She is currently implementing and evaluating ASD treatments nationally and internationally.

Robin Guenther is Principal of Perkins+Will and Senior Advisor to the non-profit Health Care Without Harm. She is a 2016 Robert Wood Johnson Foundation Culture of Health Leader. She works at the intersection of healthcare architecture and sustainable policy, and participates in a wide range of leading-edge advocacy initiatives while continuing to practise. Fast Company included her in the 2013 '100 most creative people in business'. She was a TEDMED 2014 speaker. She co-authored the book *Sustainable Healthcare Architecture* (John Wiley & Sons, 2013) and the US Department of Health and Human Services 'Sustainable and Climate Resilient Healthcare Infrastructure Toolkit'.

Charles Jencks is a renowned cultural theorist, landscape designer, architectural historian, and co-founder of the Maggie's Cancer Care Centres. His best-selling books include *The Language of Post-Modern Architecture* (Academy Editions, 1977), *Adhocism* (Secker and Warburg, 1972), *The Architecture of the Jumping Universe* (Academy Editions, 1995), and *The Architecture of Hope* (Frances Lincoln, 2010) on Maggie's Centres. His recent landscape work is summarised in *The Universe in the Landscape* (Frances Lincoln, 2011). Scotland is home to several of his most exciting landscapes including the Garden of Cosmic Speculation and Jupiter Artland, outside Edinburgh. His continuing project, the Crawick Multiverse, commissioned by the Duke of Buccleuch, culminates annually in a three-day festival of performance art and public debates with the world's leading cosmologists and scientists.

Leah Ketcheson received her doctoral degree in adapted physical activity from the School of Kinesiology, University of Michigan. She has extensive experience in the delivery and implementation of motor behavioural interventions for individuals with special needs across the lifespan. She currently teaches at Wayne State University in Detroit, and is the Director of Operations at LightUp, a non-profit organisation aimed at improving the quality of life of individuals with disabilities.

Sylvia Leydecker studied interior architecture at the University of Applied Sciences in Wiesbaden, Germany, and at Trisakti University in Jakarta. With her studio 100% interior she is working on corporate and healthcare interiors, creating wellbeing for patients and staff. She is the author of a number of books on interior architecture and materials. Her work is focused on a conceptual approach. She worked internationally for Deutsche Lufthansa before beginning her professional career as a creative. She is an honorary past board member of the International Federation of Interior Architects/Designers, and serves as Vice-President for the German Association of Interior Architects (BDIA).

Victoria Lockhart is a senior specialist at Arup, with a focus on promoting health and wellbeing through the built environment. She is a LEED AP, BREEAM AP and WELL AP, bringing expertise in sustainable green building practices alongside a passion for leveraging technology to enhance wellbeing and human experience. Her experience spans consultancy on projects across commercial, residential and industrial sectors, as well as research and advocacy for regenerative, net-positive sustainable design. More recently, she has focused on enhancing social sustainability approaches and metrics through a refocus on people, human behaviours, wellbeing and happiness.

Corbett Lyon is a founding director of Lyons, a multi-award-winning architectural design practice based in Melbourne. Lyon's notable works include the John Curtin School of Medical Research at the Australian National University and the recently completed Lady Cilento Children's Hospital in Brisbane. He is a Professorial Fellow and Visiting Professor in Design at the University of Melbourne. He lectures nationally and internationally on design and innovation, and has pioneered new methodologies for engaging stakeholders in the planning and design of public buildings, including major healthcare facilities.

Alisdair McGregor is an Arup Fellow, and principal in Arup's San Francisco office. A leader in the field of sustainable design, he is proactive in searching for environmentally sound solutions that help in the design of intelligent buildings and communities and make as small a demand as possible on the environment and its resources. He is a co-author of *Two Degrees: The Built Environment and Our Changing Climate* (Routledge, 2012).

Jeffrey Mansfield is a designer and researcher with MASS Design Group. His work has been published and presented internationally, including at MoMA PS1, the Sharjah Biennial, São Paulo Biennale, and the Bergen Assembly.

Richard Mazuch is an architect and Director of Design Research & Innovation at the design and technology firm IBI Group. A healthcare design specialist, his vast international portfolio ranges from polyclinics to complex acute hospitals, mental health facilities and hospices. He has collaborated with the Design Council, Government Treasury Task Force, Department of Health, NHS, Kings Fund and Princes' Foundation within expert working groups as consultant, advisor and author of healthcare design guidelines. As founder of IBI TH!NK, he has developed unique design tools, including Sense Sensitive Design, Design Prescription and Emotional Mapping. He is a World Architecture jury member, a university lecturer/examiner and a speaker at international conferences.

Terry Montgomery is a founding partner of Montgomery Sisam Architects with over 40 years' experience in the design of a wide range of institutional buildings. A leader in designing for clients with unique needs, he is pioneering new models in health services for youth, adults and seniors, balancing operational efficiency with a more holistic sense of wellbeing for clients, staff and families. His notable projects include the Southdown Institute, St John's Rehab at Sunnybrook Health Sciences and the Holland Bloorview Kids Rehabilitation Hospital, for which he received the Circle of Honour Award in 2009. His current projects include a major addition to Greenwood College School in Toronto, and an addition and renovation to the Waterloo Lutheran Seminary at Wilfrid Laurier University in Waterloo, Ontario.

Michael Murphy is the Executive Director and Founder of MASS Design Group, an architecture and design collaborative that leverages buildings and the design and construction process as catalysts for economic growth, social change and justice. MASS's work has been recognised globally, most recently as winners of the 2015 Design Biennial Boston, the Architectural League of New York's Emerging Voices Award and the Curry Stone Design Prize, and as finalists for the Aga Khan Award for Architecture. Murphy regularly lectures on architecture and healthcare, and teaches a course on the history of the hospital at the Harvard University Graduate School of Design (GSD).

Sunand Prasad is cofounder of the London-based architects Penoyre & Prasad. The practice's diverse range of work has won around a hundred awards and has been widely published. It is recognised for its pioneering work in healthcare and educational environments, and on sustainable design. Prasad was President of the Royal Institute of British Architects (RIBA) from 2007 to 2009. He is chairman of Article 25, the disaster relief and development charity, a member of the Board of the UK Green Building Council, and of the Editorial Board of the *Journal of Architecture*. He is the author of a number of books, articles and broadcasts on architecture, culture and sustainability.

Stephen Verderber is an architect, professor, and Associate Dean for Research at the Daniels Faculty of Architecture, Landscape, and Design at the University of Toronto. He is founding co-principal of the alternative firm Research to Architecture (R-2ARCH), and the recipient of numerous awards. He has taught and lectured at universities in North America, Asia and Europe, and has published seven books and nearly a hundred scholarly articles. His research, scholarship and professional practice explore the history and theory of design therapeutics and human/ecological health promotion.

Julian Weyer is a partner at CF Møller Architects, one of Scandinavia's leading architectural firms with over 90 years of award-winning work in the Nordic countries and worldwide, including the National Gallery in Copenhagen, the Akershus University Hospital in Oslo, and the 2012 Athletes Village for the London 2012 Olympics. He has extensive experience in the field of architecture, landscape architecture and urban design, including numerous competition wins and award-winning site-specific designs combined with sustainable, innovative and socially responsible design solutions. He is currently working on projects in Denmark, Germany and the UK as well as worldwide. He also lectures internationally, and is the author of many articles and book publications.

What is Architectural Design?

Founded in 1930, *Architectural Design* (Δ) is an influential and prestigious publication. It combines the currency and topicality of a newsstand journal with the rigour and production qualities of a book. With an almost unrivalled reputation worldwide, it is consistently at the forefront of cultural thought and design.

Each title of Δ is edited by an invited Guest-Editor, who is an international expert in the field. Renowned for being at the leading edge of design and new technologies, Δ also covers themes as diverse as architectural history, the environment, interior design, landscape architecture and urban design.

Provocative and pioneering, Δ inspires theoretical, creative and technological advances. It questions the outcome of technical innovations as well as the far-reaching social, cultural and environmental challenges that present themselves today.

For further information on Δ, subscriptions and purchasing single issues see:

www.architectural-design-magazine.com

Volume 86 No 2
ISBN 978 1118 736166

Volume 86 No 3
ISBN 978 1118 972465

Volume 86 No 4
ISBN 978 1118 951057

Volume 86 No 5
ISBN 978 1118 954980

Volume 86 No 6
ISBN 978 1119 099581

Volume 87 No 1
ISBN 978 1119 097129